All About Ground Covers

*Created and designed
by the editorial staff
of Ortho Books*

---

*Edited by
Ken Burke*

---

*Written and researched
by
Don Dimond
Michael MacCaskey*

---

*Graphic design by
Jacqueline Jones*

Ortho Books

Publisher
Robert L. Iacopi

Editorial Director
Min S. Yee

Managing Editors
Anne Coolman
Michael D. Smith

System Manager
Mark Zielinski

Senior Editor
Sally W. Smith

Editors
Jim Beley
Diane Snow
Deni Stein

System Assistant
William F. Yusavage

Production Manager
Laurie Sheldon

Photographers
Laurie A. Black
Michael D. McKinley

Photo Editors
Anne Dickson-Pederson
Pam Peirce

Production Editor
Alice E. Mace

Production Assistant
Darcie S. Furlan

National Sales Manager
Garry P. Wellman

Operations/Distribution
William T. Pletcher

Operations Assistant
Donna M. White

Administrative Assistant
Georgiann Wright

Address all inquiries to:
Ortho Books
Chevron Chemical Company
Consumer Products Division
575 Market Street
San Francisco, CA 94105

Chevron Chemical Company
575 Market Street, San Francisco, CA 94105

Acknowledgments

American Ivy Society,
Mt. Vernon, VA

Calloway Gardens,
Pine Mountain, GA

Canadian Department of
Agricultural Research,
Research Station, Summerland,
British Columbia

Classic Ground Covers,
Athens, GA

J. W. Couperthwaite,
Dallas Nurseries Garden Center,
Dallas, TX

Cunningham Gardens,
Waldron, IN

Raymond T. Entenmann,
Lambert Landscape Co.,
Dallas, TX

Morgan "Bill" Evans,
landscape architect,
Malibu, CA

Barbara Fealy, landscape architect,
Beaverton, OR

Allen C. Haskell,
New Bedford, MA

Edith Henderson, landscape architect,
Atlanta, GA

Carl McCord, Landscape Design &
Construction Co.,
Dallas, TX

McDonald's Nursery,
Walnut Creek, CA

Mannings Heather Farm,
Sebastapol, CA

Monrovia Nursery Co.,
Azusa, CA

Mountain View Nursery,
Calgary, Canada

Planting Fields Arboretum, Oyster Bay,
Long Island, NY

Rancho Santa Ana Botanic Garden,
Claremont, CA

Royal Botanical Garden,
Hamilton, Ontario

Fritz Schaeffer, Atlantic Nurseries,
Long Island, NY

Sidney Shore,
TORO,
Minneapolis, MN

Robert L. Ticknor, North Willamette
Experiment Station, OR

Russell H. Ireland, Jr.,
Martin Viette Nurseries,
East Norwich, Long Island, NY

Herb Warren,
Buchart Gardens,
British Columbia

Carl Zannger,
American Garden Perry's,
La Puente, CA

Photographers

(Names of photographers, in
alphabetical order, are followed by
page numbers on which their work
appears. R = right, L = left, T = top,
and B = bottom.)

William C. Aplin: 9TB, 10T, 13, 22T, 32, 35,
49TB, 68BR, 74TR, 77B, 78BR, 81BL, 83TR,
86B

Martha Baker: 11B

Tom Bradley: 4

Josephine Coatsworth: 44T, 73B

David Cross: 47BL, 60B, 62TL, 66B

Bill Cunningham: 18

Derek Fell: 20, 40TR, 41TB, 44B, 47TBR,
48B, 50TB, 51TR, 52TB, 56TR, 58T, 59TBR,
61B, 66TLR, 70, 72B, 73T, 77T, 80B, 83TL,
85T, 87T, 88BLR, 90B, 91BR

Pamela Harper: 10B, 11T, 33T, 37, 40BLR,
43BR, 54, 55, 56TLB, 57TB, 59BL, 60TR,
62B, 64TB, 65, 69T, 71, 74TL, 75TBL, 76T,
79B, 80T, 81BR, 82TB, 85BR, 86TL, 92B

Michael Landis: 1, 7T, 14, 31, 33B, 34T, 39,
57B, 60TL, 63T, 68T, 72T, 74B, 75BR, 76BR,
78TBL, 81T, 83B
Michael McKinley: 3, 5, 8, 21, 23, 30, 36,
43TL, 45TBL, 46T, 51TL, 53 (all), 58B, 62TR,
67TB, 69B, 86TR, 87B, 88T, 89B, 91TBL

Jack Napton: 48TR

George Taloumis: 6, 24TB, 42T, 43TR, 46B,
51B, 79T, 84T, 89T, 90T, 93B

Tom Tracy: 25

Developmental Editor

Linda Gunnarson

Illustrations

Barbara Hack

Design Assistants

Janet Theurer, Nancy Walker

Typography

George Lithograph
San Francisco, CA

Color Separations

Colorscan
Mountain View, CA

Front cover

Vinca minor under oak tree (Ortho
Photo Collection).

Back cover

Clockwise from upper left: *Campanula
poscharskyana* (photo by Michael
McKinley), *Hosta undulata* (photo by
Michael McKinley), *Potentilla verna*
(photo by William C. Aplin), and
Helianthemum 'Fire Dragon' (photo by
Pamela Harper).

Title page

Vincas, cotoneaster, and pink dianthus
provide a rich and varied understory for
small trees.

All About Ground Covers

The Most Versatile Landscape Plants

Ground covers are the practical plants of the landscape—the problem solvers—and are used to integrate and accent the other elements of a home garden. But to fully appreciate them, look beyond their obvious function to the unique beauty of color, form, and texture they can add to any location. They are truly the most versatile plants in the landscape.

Imagine a tree-shaded bed of rich green pachysandra or a cool carpet of heart-shaped violets bordering a walkway. Picture a steep slope blanketed in steel blue juniper or bright green Algerian ivy. Envision the gentle colors and textures created by a bed of mondo grass blending into a lawn. These are just a few of the uses for the versatile plants known as ground covers—plants that creep, clump, mat, or vine to cover, conceal, protect, and beautify the soil.

Ground covers include all kinds of plants—low-growing perennials, shrubs, familiar herbs, and sprawling vines— and are valued for their ability to spread rapidly, grow close to the ground, and create a thick, low-maintenance covering that binds the soil. They can be deciduous or evergreen, broad-leafed or needle-leafed, ranging in size from plants a few inches high to shrubs that reach three or more feet. Generally, the smaller the plant, the more versatile it is as a ground cover—this book is concerned primarily with low-growing plants up to about eighteen inches.

Right: A low border of ground cover violets helps delineate a garden pathway.

Opposite page: Soft to the touch and relaxing to the eyes, baby's-tears provide a delicate carpeting beneath other landscape plants.

THEY DO MORE THAN COVER THE GROUND

Ground covers fill a wide variety of needs in the garden. More often providing backup support for other plants than taking center stage, they frequently are underrated in their role as landscape problem solvers and beautifiers. When viewed with an imaginative eye, however, they can do much more than just cover the ground.

PROBLEM SOLVERS

When it comes to less-than-ideal growing conditions or problematic terrain, ground covers can provide the solution. They can be substituted for lawns where grasses cannot thrive because of poor soil, dense shade, high wind, or lack of

moisture. In a heavily wooded yard, for example, where little light penetrates to the ground, ground covers native to the forest floor—including periwinkle, wintercreeper, and goutwood—are the answer. For dry conditions, look to plants that require little water: cotoneaster, juniper, and ivy all are drought-resistant. There's a ground cover to suit any type of soil: sandy, clay, acid, alkaline, moist, or dry. Most of the herb covers—such as dwarf rosemary or creeping thyme—do well in poor soil.

Problems posed by specific landscape features also can be remedied. Ground covers can blanket and conceal a harshly angled slope or fill in a hard-to-mow space at the base of a tree. A thick ground cover planting can reduce

Right: Mountain rock cress demonstrates why it makes an ideal nook-and-cranny plant.

Opposite page: A planting of lily-of-the-valley solves the problem of mowing around the base of a tree. In the background, ivy adds color and interest to a stone wall.

Below: The purple plumes of bugleweed and the ever-green foliage of periwinkle guide strollers down a path.

maintenance under trees because the litter from leaves, flowers, fruit, or bark quietly vanishes into and beneath the cover. These materials eventually break down and enrich the soil, to the benefit of both the tree and the ground cover.

Ground covers are ideal for preventing erosion on steep slopes, where maintenance is difficult. Planting areas such as freeway banks are difficult and even dangerous to maintain, and it's in areas like these that the ground cover workhorses—ivies, junipers, honeysuckle, and vincas—really shine. They create appealing carpets while controlling erosion. They cover the land quickly and do not require frequent watering or maintenance.

The small-leafed ground covers can be used to creep into all sorts of nooks and crannies—between the cracks in garden paths, around steppingstones, in and over stone walls and fences, in any empty corner, between the exposed roots of trees, or almost any other in-between, out-of-the-way, bare spot. Tall-growing or vining types are useful for covering rocks or hiding unsightly areas. Other ground covers serve as barriers or help to direct foot traffic. Whatever the landscape problem, there's a ground cover to solve it.

Left: Don't overlook the ornamental value of ground covers. Here, the brilliant red flowers of astilbe are the focal point of a front yard.

Opposite top: A planting of mondo grass blends with a traditional grass lawn to create a relaxing, harmonious landscape.

Opposite bottom: Bands of sweet alyssum and Scotch and Irish moss add a pleasing color and texture contrast to rough-hewn wood.

BEAUTIFIERS

Although ground covers are used most frequently as problem solvers in landscapes with difficult growing conditions, they also should be considered for nonproblematic locations because of their beauty and ornamental value. The brilliant flowers of many ground covers are a special bonus, and the herbal covers offer fragrant foliage as well. Some plants provide uniform foliage color throughout the year—juniper, for example—while others, such as hostas, die back, supplying foliage color only from spring to fall.

Ground covers create harmony in a landscape. They provide a continuity of coverage that creates a feeling of tranquility. Mondo grass, for instance, serves as a pleasing transition between a lawn area and a flower bed. Besides unifying a landscape, ground covers can emphasize its patterns and forms. They offer variety in height, texture, and color that make a more exciting contribution to a setting than grass. *Potentilla verna*, with its small, yellow flowers and dark green foliage, serves as a colorful alternative to a grass lawn. Small-leafed plants such as baby's-tears and lemon thyme, which hug the ground and creep between cracks and crevices, can soften the edges of bricks or stonework and help to blend garden paths into the rest of the landscape.

Ground covers also make attractive accent plants and can be used to highlight other landscape elements. Used in combination, they create variety in depth and texture. The glossy leaves of ivy contrast interestingly with the soft, blue gray, matte effect of juniper. Scotch moss and sweet alyssum add pleasing color and texture contrasts to weathered wood. There's no limit to the imaginative combinations that can be designed to create a more appealing home landscape.

HOW TO USE THIS BOOK

This book is designed to help you choose the best ground covers to enhance your home landscape. It provides you with all the practical information you need to successfully grow hardy, attractive plants and focuses on the special problems and considerations with ground covers. But, just as importantly, it is designed to help you think creatively about the diverse landscaping possibilities ground covers offer.

To start you off, "Ground Cover Basics" presents the practical information you need to grow healthy ground cover plants. It details the essential steps, from choosing the most appropriate plant and planting time to soil preparation, fertilizing, mulching, propagating, and ongoing maintenance. It also tells you how to control pests and diseases, and—of particular importance with ground covers—how to deal with weed problems.

For a short course in using ground covers to their best advantage, turn to "Landscaping with Ground Covers." You'll discover how to use these plants on slopes, as lawn alternatives, or to drape, trail, and climb throughout your garden. To round out the course, there's stimulating advice from a gifted landscape architect, as well as a design plan and photographs of a professionally landscaped evergreen garden to help you visualize ground cover design from conception to completion.

"Using Ground Covers Imaginatively" expands on the traditional uses of ground covers in landscapes. It presents some of the more creative uses for ground covers in a home environment. If you want to experiment with ground covers as hanging plants or bonsai, in rock gardens or as topiary, you'll find practical information and imaginative examples to further inspire your creativity.

Finally, the "Plant Selection Guide" lists more than two hundred of the most widely used ground covers. In addition to a description and photographs of each plant, you'll find specific information on its culture and uses to help you choose the plants best suited to your needs.

Above: Finely textured mounds of blooming heathers create a colorful landscape.

Right: A verbena-covered mailbox provides an attractive resting place for both letters and butterflies.

Opposite top: The tall, grasslike leaves of big blue lilyturf grow between a walkway and rocks.

Opposite bottom: Gray on gray—the distinctive, light gray foliage of lavender cotton combines well with the similarly colored lamb's-ears.

Ground Cover Basics

If you set the stage carefully before planting a ground cover, and follow up with some basic care and attention, you'll be rewarded with attractive, low-maintenance plants that thrive in and enhance your home landscape.

Whether you're considering a ground cover to replace a problem lawn, cover a barren hillside, drape handsomely over a stone wall, or fill in some nooks and crannies in your garden, you'll need to understand the basic steps that are the key to growing healthy and hardy plants.

CHOOSING A GROUND COVER

Once you've decided to fill that shady corner with a ground cover, the question is, Which one? There are hundreds of possibilities. The variety in color, texture, and size is tremendous. You want a ground cover to be attractive, but even more important, it must be suitable for the particular site you want to plant. If you choose a plant simply because you like its looks, you're asking for trouble. For example, a sun-loving plant placed in a shady spot will have to be coaxed along and may never grow to your expectations. If you match the cultural requirements of the plant with the location, you're one big step ahead.

Be sure you know the growth habit, mature size, and water requirements of a ground cover before you plant it. It's

Right: Ground cover display at Arnold Arboretum in Weston, Massachusetts.

Opposite page: Stonecrop and lilyturf (foreground) with holly and garden rocks—attractive, low-maintenance choices for a pondside location.

possible to experiment with different plants for different locations; ground covers are a highly adaptable group. But if it's a problem-solving job you're asking a ground cover to fill, you probably want fast and reliable results.

Use the descriptions and photographs in the "Plant Selection Guide" to become familiar with some of the many plants available and how to grow them. Then select a ground cover that best suits your needs.

WHEN TO PLANT

The time to plant a ground cover varies across the country. In warm areas, ground covers can be planted almost anytime if water is available to see young plants through their establishment period. Generally, either a spring or fall planting is best. These are the times of least environmental stress, when the shock of transplanting is most easily endured. Temperatures are moderate and rainfall is most abundant.

In cold-winter areas, spring is usually more successful. Fall plantings are most likely to suffer from the "heaving" caused by alternate freezing and thawing of the soil. Young plants may be literally pushed out of the ground. With their roots exposed, they quickly die. If you must plant in fall, do it as early as possible to allow the young plants to become further established.

Where freezing soil is not a problem, a fall planting allows the plants to use winter rains and cool temperatures to become adjusted to their new home. And when spring comes, they are already established and begin to cover the ground more quickly. In dry-summer areas, you should avoid planting in midsummer, unless you're prepared to spend a lot of time watering.

A freshly planted bed of pachysandra. Note the uniform spacing between the plants.

PREPARING THE SOIL

Ground covers are plants that naturally grow in very close proximity, creating severe competition for space, nutrients, and water. A good soil helps overcome these adverse conditions. As a rule, soil for ground covers should be prepared as carefully as soil for a fine lawn. The advice "Don't try to live with unfavorable soil" is particularly true when planting ground covers. Extra effort in preparing the soil often makes the difference between success and failure.

Good soil can almost be equated with good drainage—for good reason. When water replaces the air in the soil, roots suffocate. Roots will not develop without a constant supply of oxygen and moisture and a constant removal of carbon dioxide.

Sandy soils are well drained but dry out quickly. Frequent watering eventually washes nutrients through the soil. Clay soils retain water and prevent air from getting to the roots.

The only quick way to improve either a sandy or heavy clay soil is through the addition of organic matter. Not just a little but lots of it. By adding organic matter—peat moss, compost, manure—clay soils are loosened up, allowing air into the soil, and they are easier to work. In light, sandy soils, organic matter holds moisture and nutrients in the root zone.

The quantity of organic matter must be large enough to physically alter the structure of the soil. "Enough" means that about one third of the final mix is organic matter. In planting terms, this would be a layer of matter spread over the soil at least 2 inches thick, worked into the soil to a depth of 6 inches.

It's not practical to go out and spade up an entire hillside and add the soil amendments. Besides the cost and time involved, the soil becomes more vulnerable to erosion. One solution is to dig a planting pocket for each plant and fill it with amended soil. This helps the plants get off to a good start.

FERTILIZING

In addition to building up the soil with amendments, an all-purpose fertilizer should be added when you prepare the planting bed. The first step in using fertilizer is understanding the labels on bags and packages.

All commercial fertilizers are labeled with the percentages of nitrogen, phosphorus, and potassium they contain.

There are many formulas, but the listings are always in the same order, with nitrogen first, phosphorus second, and potassium third. A 5–10–10 or 10–10–10 fertilizer worked into the soil before planting will get the plants off to a strong start. Spread dry fertilizers evenly over the soil (this can be done when you add the amendments) at the rate called for on the fertilizer bag; then work them in with a spade or rototiller. A normal amount would be 4 to 5 pounds of a 5–10–10

SPACING GUIDE FOR GROUND COVERS

INCHES BETWEEN PLANTS	SQUARE FEET 64 PLANTS WILL COVER	SQUARE FEET 100 PLANTS WILL COVER
4	7	11
6	16	25
8	28	44
10	45	70
12	64	100
15	100	156
18	144	225
24	256	400

FORMULAS TO DETERMINE SQUARE FEET:
CIRCLES: Area = diameter squared × 0.7854
TRIANGLES: Area = 1/2 base × height
RECTANGLES: Area = base × height

fertilizer per 100 square feet. Many fertilizers supply additional elements, such as iron and zinc, that may be lacking in the soil, some in very minute amounts. If you've had the soil tested, the analysis will help you determine which fertilizer to use and how much. If you haven't tested your soil, a complete, all-purpose fertilizer will satisfy most plants' requirements.

PLANTING

There's no hard and fast rule in estimating the number of plants for a given location. The spacing chart on this page is provided by American Garden Perry's, a California ground cover grower. It will give you an idea of how many plants you need. The number also depends on the effect you want to achieve, how fast you want the effect, and the funds you have available. Naturally, the closer you space the plants, the faster they will cover the ground completely.

As a guide, such plants as English ivy, pachysandra, and periwinkle are planted on 1-foot centers; cranberry cotoneaster, junipers, and euonymus on 3-foot centers. Trailing roses, Virginia creeper, and other large-scale ground covers are often spaced no closer than 5 feet.

Some woody plants, such as junipers, will eventually mound up if they have been planted too closely. If you must space the plants close together to achieve a more immediate effect, be prepared to remove some at a later time.

Spacing differs with the location. If you are planting a small area by your front door, you probably won't want to wait two years for it to fill in. The most immediate effect (and the most expensive) would be a ground cover that could be rolled out just like a sod lawn. Many ground cover plants cannot be handled in this way, but some, including the widely used English ivy, can. A number of growers are having success with the sod method.

In arranging the plants, some gardeners opt for staggered rows, others for straight. One advantage of staggered row planting on slopes is that it helps prevent erosion by not allowing water to run off in a straight line.

When planting on slopes, it is necessary to hold the soil in place until the plants themselves can do the job. A mulch alone is sufficient in most cases. When the slope is steep, use jute or a similar netting to hold the mulch in place. Jute is usually available in rolls 4 or 6 feet wide. Unroll the netting from the top of the hill and hold it in place with heavy-wire staples (coat hangers are easily adaptable to this use).

A recently planted slope, particularly one without a mulch, is more difficult to water than a planting in a level area. There is the constant threat of erosion. Creating small terraces around each plant or terraces across the width of the slope can help control runoff. If erosion occurs, apply the water more slowly. Drip systems are best for watering. Mist or fine-spray sprinklers also can be used. Another method is to "cycle water"—meaning leave the sprinklers on for 10 minutes (or until the water runs off) and then off for 20 minutes, giving the water time to soak in. Repeat this until the soil is thoroughly soaked.

THE PROBLEM OF WEEDS

Weeds can quickly overrun any planting and turn an enthusiastic gardener into a frustrated one. The most critical time is just after planting, particularly if in the spring. You'll need to keep a close eye on newly planted ground covers until they are dense enough to shade the ground and choke out weeds.

If a weed problem is severe, drastic treatment may be necessary. If the area to be planted is heavily infested with perennial or hard-to-stop weeds such as quackgrass, Bermuda grass, milkweed, and bindweed, fumigate the soil after it is prepared and ready to plant. Some landscape and pest-control companies offer this service, or you can do it yourself. Vapam is commonly available to home gardeners and will dramatically reduce the number of weeds in your soil.

Mulches (see below) applied on a new planting will help stave off the weed population. They should be applied only after the soil has warmed in the spring. A generous quantity (3 to 5 inches thick) will stop many of the most troublesome annual weeds and make it easier to pull out the ones that do sprout.

Get in the habit of taking a walk through your garden or newly planted area about once a week, taking a bag and weeding tool along. Place all pulled weeds in the bag; if left on the ground they can reroot or spread seeds.

Preemergent herbicides containing Treflan or Dacthal will considerably reduce weed problems. For successful weed control using preemergent-type herbicides, read and follow directions carefully. In established plantings, the post-emergent Dowpon will control grassy weeds such as Bermuda grass without harming the ground cover. The label lists ground covers on which it can be used safely.

Finally, if you desire further information about these or other methods of weed control, talk to an agricultural extension agent or local nursery people. They can tell you about weeds and control methods specific to your area.

MULCHES

A good, weed-free mulch is a most valuable addition to a new ground cover planting. A couple of inches of mulch will keep weeds down and make them easier to pull out if they do appear; 4 to 5 inches will prevent most weeds from growing. Some of the better mulches are sawdust, fir bark, ground bark, and tree leaves, as well as gravel and rocks. There are many others of limited availability, depending upon your region.

Besides preventing weeds from growing, some organic mulches improve the soil and add nutrients as they decompose. They also conserve moisture, an important consideration where summertime water is in short supply and anytime young, shallow-rooted plants are just getting started. Finally, soil temperature is controlled evenly, creating a more favorable root environment.

You also might try a living mulch of flowering annuals while the ground cover is filling in. It will hide the bare spots with color.

In some harsh-winter areas, some ground covers benefit from a winter mulch. A mulch applied at the time of a new fall planting will prolong the time it takes the soil to freeze, allowing plants to become further established.

MULCHING MATERIALS

SAWDUST, WOOD CHIPS, WOOD SHAVINGS
Low in plant nutrients, decompose slowly, tend to pack down. Well-rotted material preferred. Can be fresh if nitrate of ammonia or nitrate of soda is supplemented at the rate of 1 pound per 100 square feet. Keep away from building foundations; may cause termites.

PEAT MOSS
Attractive, available, but expensive for large areas. Should be kept moist at all times.

ROTTED MANURE
May contain weed seeds.

MUSHROOM COMPOST (SPENT)
Often available in areas where commercial mushrooms are produced. Usually inexpensive, with a good color that blends into the landscape.

SHREDDED HARDWOOD BARK
Makes an excellent mulch that is easy to apply and very attractive. Lasts longer than peat moss; adds valuable organic matter to the soil.

PINE NEEDLES
Will not mat down. Fairly durable.

TREE LEAVES (WHOLE OR SHREDDED)
Excellent source of humus. Rot rapidly; high in nutrients. Oak leaves especially valuable for azaleas, camellias, and rhododendrons.

GROUND CORN COBS
Excellent for improving soil structure.

GRAVEL, STONE CHIPS
Limited use, but particularly good for rock garden plantings. Extremely durable, hold down weeds, but do not supply plant nutrients or humus.

HAY, GRASS CLIPPINGS
Unattractive, but repeated use builds up reserve of available nutrients that lasts for years.

STRAW
Same as for "Hay, Grass Clippings" but lower in nutrients, although furnishes considerable potassium.

BARK
Ground and packaged commercially. Especially attractive in this form. Sometimes available in rough form from pulpwood loading sites.

With an established ground cover, apply the mulch *after* the ground is frozen, to keep it that way. Damage occurs when the soil alternately thaws and freezes. A loosely applied mulch such as straw or shredded leaves over the ground cover also insulates plants against drying winter winds. Air should be able to circulate around the foliage.

PROPAGATING

Occasionally your bed or slope of ground cover will develop a bare spot, or you may want to extend a planting into a new area. Try some "preventive propagation" at home so that you can fill in those inevitable bare places as soon as they occur.

The three most common methods of propagating ground cover plants are division, cuttings, and layering. For the average gardener, division is the simplest method. All you have to do is divide clumps of established plants, spacing individual plants in the area you want them to cover.

Gardening purists may prefer to extend their plants by cuttings. Some use shady, out-of-the-way spots to propagate cuttings, always having a few flats ready for repairing planting beds. Softwood cuttings are most frequently used for cutting-propagated ground covers. To know if a twig is at this stage, bend it. It's at the right point if it readily snaps in two.

Place the cuttings into a flat or container holding a moistened, sterile medium (potting soil, vermiculite, perlite, etc.). A hormone powder (available in retail outlets) applied on the tips of the cuttings will help in rooting. A greenhouse or coldframe is the ideal location for storing the flats. Otherwise, find a shady, humid, sheltered area, keeping the rooting medium moist at all times.

Plants vary in how long they need to grow roots. Check the cuttings after a couple of weeks—if roots are too small or not visible yet, just tuck the cuttings back into place.

To propagate by layering, you root stems or branches while they are still attached to the mother plant. Many ground covers—English ivy, for example—layer naturally. Spring is the best time to start layers. To layer a plant, simply tie, stake, or otherwise hold the stem you want layered down to the soil. Mound several inches of soil over the lowest point and keep the area moist.

ELIMINATING THE MYTH OF NO MAINTENANCE

Presently, ground covers are mistakenly thought of as no-maintenance plants. This philosophy pervades all areas of ground cover culture: in the preparation of a location, and in watering, fertilizing, and pruning. Perhaps because ground covers are the problem solvers—growing in areas where a lawn wouldn't be found—they are often allotted second-class status. But ground covers have the same fundamental needs as any plant.

There are, of course, ground covers that can grow in less than ideal soil; still others that can grow on a steep slope better than anywhere else. But ground covers deserve your best efforts. Even if you give them just half the attention you give your lawn, you'll be happily surprised at the results. Given adequate care, they blanket the ground with striking color or foliage (doing the job they're supposed to do) instead of just barely covering it.

WATERING

Young plants should be given special attention. A steady watering program is important so that root systems develop fully. There is no rule such as "Water once a week in the summer"—there are too many variations. You have to watch the plants and make sure water is getting to the roots. After the plants are growing, your program should be adjusted to one of deeper and less frequent watering. This causes the roots to go further down into the soil. Plants then become firmly entrenched in the ground, and in a drought situation this could make the difference in the survival of your ground cover.

Use a sprinkler to water. Hand watering is all right in many situations, but it is too easy to overestimate the time you've been watering and equally easy to become satisfied when everything appears to be well wetted. There is no substitute for a thorough watering. If water is scarce in your area, consider a drip-irrigation system.

Interplanting with annuals while a ground cover is filling in provides a colorful mulch against weeds. Here, sweet alyssum combines with Algerian ivy.

Check the soil for adequate moisture. To do this by hand, simply dig down to root depth and get a handful of soil. If it won't form a ball, it's most likely too dry. If it forms a ball that doesn't crumble easily, it's probably too wet. (Sandy soil crumbles even when it is too wet.) A simple way to test the soil is with a moisture meter. There are many different brands available. Choose a sturdy model with a long probe for outdoor use.

MOWING

You probably expected to leave your lawn mower in the garage when you planted ground covers. But there is one consolation: ground covers need to be mowed only to rejuvenate new growth, usually just once a year.

Mowing, or any method of cutting back old growth, is very important to the appearance of a ground cover. As with watering, there is no firm schedule to abide by. When a ground cover is beginning to thatch, or the foliage loses its fresh look, it's time to clip off the old growth. Generally, the best time to trim is just prior to the plant's normal growth cycle. This would be in spring for most ground covers, just as the weather begins to warm.

There are several methods of trimming, depending on the size and location of the ground cover. Bill Cunningham, a wholesale grower of ground covers in Indiana, devised the mower on stilts shown in the photograph on this page. He reports:

"With mowing, we've reduced maintenance costs and work time and eliminated the burden of hand pruning. Then, too, mowing enhances the beauty of carpeting plants; some of the taller-growing, vining types *must* be pruned for the preferred, orderly appearance. As far as I know, none of the mower manufacturers has rigged the rotaries for clipping at, say, 4-inch, 6-inch, or 8-inch heights. In working

this out for our program, we settled on the mower shown because the wheels were in line, simplifying the mounting of wheels on so-called stilts. We used 1-inch square tubing for the additional height needed, drilling holes in the steel for adjusting to required heights. A mower equipped with a bag for collecting the clipping debris is necessary. We do know euonymus, pachysandra, *Phlox subulata*, and ajuga can be controlled in this way. I'm sure there are many other plants that benefit from mowing. We feel there is no better, faster, labor-saving way."

Weeds may appear in a ground cover after it was been mowed. This happens when soil and weed seeds that have long been covered are suddenly exposed. If you mow a ground cover so low that bare soil is exposed, use a preemergent herbicide as discussed under "The problem of weeds" earlier in this chapter. Before applying the herbicide, check the label to see if your ground cover is tolerant of it.

TRIMMING SLOPES

But how do you mow an inaccessible area or a steep slope? The nylon line trimmers that have become so popular for edging and trimming can be used to some extent in trimming ground covers. Depending on the toughness of the foliage and the power of your trimmer, this tool can do the job when nothing else can (aside from tedious hand-shearing). Keeping the trimmer an equal distance from the ground to maintain a level cut is a little tricky, but not a serious problem.

HAND PRUNING

Some ground covers can be improved by pruning rather than mowing. Using pruning shears on such plants as Oregon grape (*Mahonia aquifolium*) and wintergreen (*Gaultheria* species) helps to maintain compactness and desired dense growth.

PESTS AND OTHER PROBLEMS

Because ground covers are such a diverse group of plants, it is difficult to categorize their pests and diseases and the best methods of controlling them. Pests common to individual plants are listed with each ground cover's description in the "Plant Selection Guide." The chart on the following page lists pests that attack nearly all plants, including ground covers, as well as recommended methods for controlling them.

Nicknamed the "euonymus clipping machine," this modified lawn mower is invaluable for trimming large areas. For best results, ground covers should be trimmed just prior to new growth.

PESTS AND DISEASES

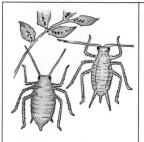

APHIDS
Aphids come in several colors and sizes. They suck plant juices, stunt growth, pucker and curl leaves, deform buds and flowers, cause galls to form, and generally make a nuisance of themselves around the garden. The systemic Orthene and the contact insecticide diazinon control aphids.

BEETLES
Beetles are a huge and diverse group of insects that includes many beneficial as well as destructive types. Damage from beetles varies greatly. Most beetles are controlled by spraying carbaryl, diazinon, or malathion.

BUGS
Bugs, to most people, mean all kinds of insects. To a gardener, "bugs" are a suborder of insects. Lace bugs are especially fond of cotoneaster. Orthene and malathion insecticides are usually ef-

fective against bugs. Be sure to cover the plant thoroughly with the spray, including the leaf undersides.

CATERPILLARS AND WORMS
Caterpillars and worms are most often the larvae of moths and butterflies. There are hundreds of kinds of these pests. All feed on foliage. Orthene, carbaryl, and the bacterial insecticide *Bacillus thuringiensis* are effective.

CROWN AND ROOT ROT
Crown and root rot are fungus diseases usually caused by too much water. Crown rot is caused by planting too deep as well as by excess water in the soil. Roots of dead plants have a putrid sulfurous odor. Improve drainage by grading, adding soil amendments, or planting in raised beds.

LEAFHOPPERS
Leafhoppers are small, usually wedge-shaped insects with piercing-sucking mouthparts. Usually they suck sap from lower leaf surfaces, causing loss of color and a stippled appearance on top surfaces. Orthene, diazinon, and malathion control these pests.

LEAF MINERS
Leaf miners are larvae of several kinds of flies, midges, and moths. When eggs hatch, they feed inside, between the leaf surfaces, creating ugly blotches or serpentine trails. The holly species arc frequent victims of leaf miners. Orthene, diazinon, and various combination sprays effectively control miners.

MEALYBUGS
Mealybugs are close relatives of scale. They may occur singly or in groups on twigs and undersides of branches, mostly in crotches. Injury occurs when large, sap-sucking populations build up. Symptoms are loss of color, loss of vigor, and wilting. Orthene, diazinon, and dormant oil plus malathion are effective against mealybugs.

MITES
Mites are not really insects, but tiny spider relatives. They damage plants by sucking sap from lower leaf surfaces, causing the top surfaces to turn pale and show a stippled appearance. Under heavy infestation, webs will appear. The insecticides malathion, diazinon, and Orthene are effective against some mites. A dormant oil

spray controls overwintering eggs of spider mites. Commonly available combination sprays containing dicofol are also effective.

SCALE
Scale is divided into two types, armored and soft. Armored scales live beneath an outer shell of molted skins and waxy secretions. The shell of the soft scale is an integral part of the scale insect, like the shell of a turtle, and though called "soft," is often as hard as armored scale. Soft scales usually secrete honeydew, causing unsightly blackening of foliage and sticky drippings on cars and walks beneath infested plants. Except when in their "crawler" stage, scales are immobile, protected from predators and most insecticides by their shell. Scale crawlers appear just after eggs hatch, usually in the spring. To control scale crawlers, spray the plant completely with Orthene or diazinon. In late fall and early spring, spray a combination of dormant oil and malathion to control mature scales and their overwintering eggs.

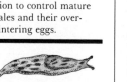

SNAILS AND SLUGS
Snails and slugs are frequent inhabitants of ground cover plantings.

If they don't damage the ground cover itself, they use it for their daytime hideout and feed on other plants at night. Expect to find these pests wherever the ground is constantly moist—that's the prerequisite of any home for these creatures. Metaldehyde and Mesurol® baits are commonly available and effective. Zectran spray controls these pests also.

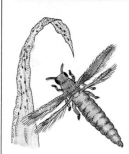

THRIPS
Thrips scrape and scar foliage and feed inside buds so that flowers become deformed or fail to open. They are brownish yellow and tiny, barely visible without a magnifying glass. Look for thrips by shaking infested flowers into your hand or over a piece of paper. Orthene, diazinon, and malathion are recommended controls.

WHITEFLIES
Whiteflies are small, pure white, and wedge-shaped. Nymphs are scalelike, flat, oval, and pale green, brown, or black, depending on the species. They do damage by sucking juices from the undersides of leaves. Orthene controls whiteflies. On some plants a dormant oil spray is effective.

Landscaping With Ground Covers

Take a close look at your home landscape. Would a ground cover
help to camouflage and stabilize an eroding slope?
Highlight the space beneath a heavy shade tree? Provide contrast
against a large expanse of lawn? This chapter presents
some guidelines and ideas for designing with ground covers,
including advice from a professional.

This chapter is designed to be a short course in
landscaping with ground covers, so that you, the
homeowner, can use these plants to their best
advantage. The first part of the chapter illustrates
the primary ways ground covers are used in
landscaping: to blanket slopes; as lawn alternatives; to
drape, trail, and climb; and to fill in nooks and crannies.
Following this, you'll find some inspiring advice from a
noted landscape architect, as well as photographs and a
design plan for a professional's evergreen garden nursery.

THE "IDEAL" LANDSCAPE

An ideal landscape could be defined as one in which the
viewer isn't aware of any one element, a setting in which a
balanced blending of diverse plant materials creates a harmonious, tranquil mood.

Ground covers are ideal for unifying a landscape. Their
variety of growth habits, foliage, color, and texture, and their
range of cultural requirements allow them to fit into any setting. Ground covers blend so well into our outdoor environment that we often take them for granted. But without this
versatile group of plants, landscapes would be starkly
incomplete.

**Right: Foamflower, wild
ginger, heron's bill, and
phlox add to the harmony
of an "ideal" woodland
landscape.**

**Opposite page: A ground
cover of crested iris high-
lights a naturalistic garden.**

Every home landscape also needs contrasts and accents to keep it from becoming monotonous. Visual focal points brought about by plant color, shape, or texture create interest in the landscape by capturing the viewer's attention. Such focal points can be achieved with individual ground cover plants or by mass plantings. A ground cover planted adjacent to a lawn will break up the expanse of green, adding interesting lines and textures. Splashes of ground cover color—including varying shades of green—against stone walls, along paths and steps, or in specimen plants will create the needed contrasts and variety.

In their role as decorative accents, ground covers also may provide practical solutions to small problem areas—for example, ajuga grouped to cover the exposed roots at the base of a tree. But be sure to use any accent plant with restraint. Too many varieties with contrasting colors and textures will create a hodgepodge rather than the integrated landscape you set out to design.

SLOPES

A slope or hillside in a home landscape can be transformed into a gardening asset. A slope offers an added vertical dimension a flat lot doesn't have. It can be terraced and tiered to eliminate erosion, providing a creative gardener with numerous planting possibilities. When planted in a ground cover, it becomes a living backdrop for color displays of interplanted bulbs, annuals, flowering shrubs, and trees.

A slope is a difficult-to-plant area, especially if it is steep; yet it is vitally important that it be protected with some type of plant cover. A bare slope is more than an eyesore; it is

in danger of being damaged by erosion. Rainfall and existing runoff wash valuable topsoil away, creating unsightly and unplantable gullies, and heavy rains can cause dangerous mudslides. Ground covers provide a practical solution for slopes.

There are quite a few ground covers that look good and also effectively protect hillsides against erosion. (See page 27 for a listing of some of the best slope stabilizers.) Most require minimal maintenance once established. Vining ground covers, such as ivy, are excellent as soil stabilizers, and their bright, shiny leaves are very attractive. Cuttings often can be planted directly on the slope. With the heavier ground covers, such as junipers, it is sometimes necessary to build individual terraces to hold the plants in position until they become established.

Erosion remains a threat until a ground cover has fully developed its foliage to cover the bare soil. In the meantime, cover the slope with netting (jute, available in retail nurseries) to stop the runoff. Drip systems are best for watering.

LAWN ALTERNATIVES

If your home is landscaped like most, it has both a front and a back yard. And, like most homes, both areas are probably carpeted with grass—for good reason. Grass is certainly the most widespread and most durable plant material used to cover the ground.

But there are situations in which grass will not grow. Or perhaps you just want to plant something different. Ground covers can provide attractive alternatives in such situations, and they have the added advantage of requiring less maintenance. Less maintenance doesn't mean no maintenance, however. Most ground covers need to be watered, fertilized, and trimmed on a regular basis to look their best—but not nearly as often as a lawn.

Before planting a ground cover as a lawn alternative (or for any reason), the soil should be prepared the same as you would for a lawn (see the chapter "Ground Cover Basics"). After a ground cover becomes established, it is extremely difficult to improve the soil since it is completely covered with foliage. A well-prepared soil before planting allows the ground cover to grown healthier and cover the ground much faster.

One of the most valuable traits of grass is its ability to accept traffic. That is why a back yard usually is planted with a grass lawn—to bear the brunt of a family's recreation. Many ground covers will take some traffic also, but not the kind delivered by active children; so they are of limited use in a back yard. But since a front lawn is usually a showcase, grown and maintained for visual rather than functional reasons, why not try a ground cover there, to provide the desired carpet of green without the maintenance that is required by a grass lawn? Ground covers offer more than grass visually— different foliage and blossom colors, as well as an array of foliage textures. For a listing of large-scale lawn alternatives, see page 27.

DRAPE, TRAIL, AND CLIMB

Some ground covers climb or trail as easily as they spread along the ground. For example, woolly thyme can be encouraged to cover an old log, and Virginia creeper can add character and color to a brick wall. Euonymus can climb to frame a doorway, and creeping Jennie can trail to fill in the nooks and crannies in a rock garden.

The idea is to look at ground covers with a discriminating eye. Is a particular plant best at eye level, or better to look up at or down upon? Carefully consider the plant's form and growth habit in terms of the vertical dimension, since what grows horizontally on the ground might do some interesting things when made to drape, twirl or climb.

Ivy is equally at home trailing down a steep slope or vining along a porch or trellis. Cotoneaster adds texture as it tumbles over a stone wall. Rosemary and carissa make good companions spilling down a garden slope.

Sometimes plant behavior takes on an interesting twist when viewed from a new angle. For instance, honeysuckle, when planted in a hanging basket and left to its own devices, may twine itself into a giant green braid. The point is to ignore whatever preconceptions you may have about ground covers and their more common horizontal use in the landscape. If you come up with a new way to use a plant, try it. Ground covers will hang, trail, drape, cascade, or sprawl; they'll twine, vine, climb, creep, or spread; they'll grow up, down, over, and out—just as many ways as you let them. (For further creative use of ground covers, see the chapter "Using Ground Covers Imaginatively.")

Above: Cotoneaster drapes naturally alongside a stone wall.

Left: Use ground covers as landscape accents. Here, the striking foliage of snow-in-summer hugs the contours of natural rock; tufts of gold-moss stonecrop provide a counterpoint.

Opposite page: Lilyturf and Korean grass create a rich, green carpet for a low-maintenance landscape.

considerations—situations where an inspired use of just the right ground covers will produce more gratifying effects.

The great range of plants suitable for ground covering tasks affords opportunities not present with turf. Sloping or rolling ground unsuited for lawn culture can be turned to distinct aesthetic advantage by playing up the grade differentials. Or, where confronted with an uninteresting level plane, motion in three dimensions can be created by the import of fill soil or sculpturing of existing earth, again to provide the subtle contours best enhanced by appropriate cover plants. In extreme cases where manmade sites present unlovely cut-and-fill slopes, rescue is possible and grade adjustment achieved with the help of boulders, stone riff-raff, railroad ties, and the correct choice of plant material. A sensitively molded earthform can be treated with the kind of cover that exactly preserves its flowing lines; or an offensive, mechanical slope can be so artfully disguised by well-chosen plantings that its shape is unseen.

The interplay of natural stone, masonry, or wood with select ground covers opens up new dimensions literally and figuratively. Steps, paths, and terraces can be crisply or subtly delineated; pebbles and bark-wood rounds are mutually complementary elements to incorporate in ground cover design solutions.

Recently developed techniques for simulating natural rock forms offer an exciting new approach in which difficult grade conditions can be converted from a vice to a virtue. The process evolved over several years and with the input of various artisans, the most successful of whom now offer custom service. Methods vary, but in general it is now possible to produce surprisingly realistic shapes and textures simulating nearly every natural rock condition—dry, or incorporating a wide variety of water effects. The final product can be purely aesthetic or functional. It can be poured in place, as a reinforced retaining wall, for example. Crevices, ledges, and planting pockets form part of the design and permit the culture of appropriate trailing plant materials for a harmonious marriage of the natural and the artificial.

It is a long design stride from the above to the simple and straightforward treatment of irregular terrain with native plants. Each region has its own indigenous plant communities, which invariably include spreading, sprawling, or creeping covers.

The best of these subjects found their way into commercial culture and catalogs long ago; hybrids and type selections have multiplied the options, in some cases to a bewildering degree (junipers, for example). But in almost every part of this land where gardening is pursued, the opportunity to cover your particular earth with essentially low-maintenance native plants is present. In the low rainfall zones of southern California and Arizona, we have had

GROUND COVER LANDSCAPING: PROFESSIONAL ADVICE

The following discussion on landscaping with ground covers is written by Morgan "Bill" Evans, of Malibu, California. Evans could be called the professional's professional; for twenty-one years he was Director of Landscape Design for Disneyland in California and Walt Disney World in Florida, and he is a past president of the American Institute of Landscape Architects. He has landscaped miniature Matterhorns and has designed life-size animal topiaries.

Nothing is more gracious or complimentary to the landscape than a great sweep of velvet grass. In some circumstances, nothing else should be considered. By the same token, however, there are many sites where grass is simply not the answer. In addition to the obvious reasons (terrain, light conditions, high maintenance), there are subtle design

to borrow from the Mediterranean, West Australia, and South Africa to supplement our rather meager native supply, but these imports have so comfortably fit into the local scene that we may be pardoned for treating them as our own.

Scale plays an important part in plant selection. This aspect is reflected not only in specific leaf size, but in habit of growth—compact versus arching; creeping or matlike as opposed to self-supporting, horizontal growth. There are plants that blend into a continuous texture for sweeping lines and plants that are most attractive as individuals.

No discussion of ground cover options would be complete without reference to the succulents. The term *succulent* is somewhat imprecise because plants so identified belong to widely divergent families; but in a broad sense, those subjects that tend to be fleshy, plump, and full of juice or sap are lumped together as succulents. They are native to an astonishing geography, from Siberia through the tropics to the tip of South America and South Africa. Although some are extremely hardy and moisture-tolerant, as a class they are best adapted to warm, dry climates where their camel-like ability to store water carries them for long periods without irrigation. Of infinite form and behavior, many are distinguished by spectacular flowers as well as attractive color tones in foliage. As with ground covers in general, the choices are legion in size, scale, posture, and performance. In the warmer sections of the country, an entire landscape design may be executed with succulents for impressive results.

We have scarcely mentioned grass since the opening paragraph, but of course there are many pleasing combinations of grass and ground cover. Some distinction should be

SELECTED PLANTS FOR SPECIAL SITUATIONS

Because ground covers display such a wide range of cultural requirements and growth habits, some are naturally better suited than others to specific landscape situations. The following lists are designed to help you choose plants to meet the particular needs of your home landscape. The lists are not exhaustive but represent some of the most common ground covers available.

EASY TO GROW

Ajuga reptans (Bugleweed)
Arctostaphylos uva-ursi (Kinnikinnick)
Baccharis pilularis 'Twin Peaks'
  (Dwarf coyote brush)
Cotoneaster
Euonymus fortunei 'Colorata' (Wintercreeper)
Hedera (Ivy)
Hypericum calycinum (Aaron's beard)
Juniperus (Juniper)
Liriope spicata (Lilyturf)
Ophiopogon japonicus (Mondo grass)
Pachysandra terminalis (Japanese spurge)
Potentilla verna (Spring cinquefoil)
Rosmarinus officinalis 'Prostratus'
  (Dwarf rosemary)
Sedum (Stonecrop)
Trachelospermum (Jasmine)
Vinca minor (Periwinkle)

DROUGHT–RESISTANT

Aegopodium podagraria (Goutweed)
Arctostaphylos uva-ursi (Kinnikinnick)
Artemisia (Dusty-miller, wormwood)
Baccharis pilularis 'Twin Peaks'
  (Dwarf coyote brush)
Cistus (Rock rose)
Coronilla varia (Crown vetch)
Cytisus (Broom)
Festuca ovina glauca (Blue fescue)
Genista (Broom)
Helianthemum nummularium (Sun rose)
Hemerocallis (Daylily)
Juniperus (Juniper)
Lantana
Phalaris arundinacea 'Picta' (Ribbon grass)
Phyla nodiflora (Lippia)
Rosmarinus officinalis 'Prostratus'
  (Dwarf rosemary)
Santolina chamaecyparissus (Lavender
  cotton)
Sedum (Stonecrop)
Verbena peruviana (Peruvian verbena)

FULL SUN

Achillea tomentosa (Woolly yarrow)
Arabis (Rock cress)
Arctostaphylos uva-ursi (Kinnikinnick)
Artemisia schmidtiana (Angel's hair)
Baccharis pilularis (Dwarf coyote brush)
Ceanothus (California lilac)
Cerastium tomentosum (Snow-in-summer)
Cotoneaster, low-growing
Cytisus (Broom)
Helianthemum nummularium (Sun rose)
Juniperus (Juniper)
Lantana
Phlox subulata (Moss pink)
Phyla nodiflora (Lippia)
Pyracantha koidzumii 'Santa Cruz'
  (Santa Cruz pyracantha)
Rosa (Rose)
Rosmarinus officinalis 'Prostratus'
  (Dwarf rosemary)
Santolina chamaecyparissus (Lavender cotton)
Sedum (Stonecrop)

SUN OR PARTIAL SHADE

Aegopodium podagraria (Goutweed)
Ajuga (Bugleweed)
Bergenia
Campanula (Bellflower)
Cyrtomium falcatum (Holly fern)
Dichondra micrantha (Dichondra)
Epimedium (Barrenwort)
Fragaria chiloensis (Wild or sand strawberry)
Hedera helix (English ivy)
Hypericum calycinum (Aaron's beard)
Liriope spicata (Lilyturf)
Mahonia repens (Creeping mahonia)
Ophiopogon japonicus (Mondo grass)
Paxistima canbyi (Canby, pachistima)
Polygonum (Knotweed)
Sagina subulata (Irish and Scotch moss)
Trachelospermum (Jasmine)

made between grasses like *Festuca ovina glauca* or *Zoysia tenuifolia* 'Aurel' and conventional turf grasses. The former are regarded as ground covers per se, whereas turf grass of whatever breed requires a special kind of maintenance absent in ground cover culture.

In so many of our contemporary architectural designs, modest expanses of trim grass, freeform or geometrical, are desirable to complement certain structural elements. Shadow patterns, including those of trees, are better revealed on lawn than on ground cover, for example. Turf and ground cover associations often flatter each other.

When a planting line is created, it is usually a good idea to keep it going as far as practicable, seeking some motion but avoiding abrupt change of direction. Tiered perspectives are attainable by the use of carefully selected species, thus adding a third dimension to a flat site.

A word of caution—whether you handle the job yourself or contract with a professional, be sure to apply a preemergent herbicide. Satisfaction can be short-lived if weeds invade. One can live with certain intruders when the grass is cut weekly, and selective weed controls are a welcome assist; but nothing is more tiresome or frustrating than battling entrenched weeds among ground covers. After the earth has been shaped and graded, after the header boards are in place and the soil has been suitably turned and amended, be sure that the correct herbicides are carefully applied. As an extra precaution, regular irrigation should be practiced for a reasonable period to coax out any fugitive weeds before the finished planting.

Good ground cover landscaping is not easy, but with some study and much prudent thought (plus honest toil), it is within reach of most home gardeners.

✓ = tolerates lots of moisture

TOLERATE DEEP SHADE

✓ *Adiantum pedatum* (Five-finger fern)
✓ *Asarum* (Wild ginger)
✓ *Athyrium goeringianum* (Japanese painted fern)
✓ *Convallaria majalis* (Lily-of-the-valley)
✓ *Dryopteris* (Wood fern)
Epimedium (Barrenwort)
✓ *Galium odoratum* (Sweet woodruff) NO TRAFFIC
Hedera helix (English ivy)
✓ *Pachysandra terminalis* (Japanese spurge)
∿ *Sagina subulata* (Irish and Scotch moss)
✓ *Sarcococca hookeriana humilis* (Small Himalayan sarcococca)
✓ *Viola odorata* (Sweet violet)

LAWN ALTERNATIVES (LARGE AREAS)

Aegopodium podagraria (Goutweed)
Ajuga reptans (Bugleweed)
Arctostaphylos uva-ursi (Kinnikinnick)
Baccharis pilularis 'Twin Peaks' (Dwarf coyote brush)
Coronilla varia (Crown vetch)
Dianthus deltoides (Maiden pink)
Dichondra
Duchesnea indica (Mock strawberry)
Euonymus fortunei (Wintercreeper)
Festuca ovina glauca (Blue fescue)
Fragaria chiloensis (Wild or sand strawberry)
Hedera (Ivy)
Hypericum calycinum (Aaron's beard)
Juniperus (Juniper, low-growing)
Lantana
Liriope spicata (Lilyturf)
Lonicera japonica (Honeysuckle)
Pachysandra terminalis (Japanese spurge)
Phyla nodiflora (Lippia)
Polygonum cuspidatum compactum (Fleece flower)
Potentilla (Cinquefoil)
Sedum (Stonecrop)
Trachelospermum (Jasmine)
Vinca (Periwinkle)
Zoysia tenuifolia (Korean grass)

SLOPE STABILIZERS

Akebia quinata (Five-leaf akebia)
Arctostaphylos uva-ursi (Kinnikinnick)
Baccharis pilularis 'Twin Peaks' (Dwarf coyote brush)
Ceanothus griseus horizontalis (Carmel creeper)
Cistus (Rock rose)
Coronilla varia (Crown vetch)
Cotoneaster, low-growing
Hedera (Ivy)
Hemerocallis (Daylily)
Hypericum calycinum (Aaron's beard)
Juniperus (Juniper, low-growing)
Lantana montevidensis (Lantana)
Lonicera (Honeysuckle)
Lotus berthelotii (Parrot's-beak)
Parthenocissus quinquefolia (Virginia creeper)
Phalaris arundinacea 'Picta' (Ribbon grass)
Polygonum cuspidatum compactum (Fleece flower)
Pyracantha koidzumii 'Santa Cruz' (Santa Cruz pyracantha)
Rosa (Rose, low-growing)
Rosmarinus officinalis 'Prostratus' (Dwarf rosemary)
Vinca (Periwinkle)

DRAPE AND TRAIL

Arctostaphylos uva-ursi (Kinnikinnick)
Artemisia (Dusty-miller, wormwood)
Asparagus densiflorus 'Sprengeri' (Sprenger asparagus fern)
Campanula (Bellflower)
Cerastium tomentosum (Snow-in-summer)
Cotoneaster, low-growing
Euonymus fortunei (Euonymus, in variety)
Hedera (Ivy)
Juniperus (Juniper, low-growing)
Lotus berthelotii (Parrot's-beak)
Rosmarinus officinalis 'Prostratus' (Dwarf rosemary)
Trachelospermum jasminoides (Star jasmine)
Verbena peruviana (Peruvian verbena)
Vinca minor (Perwinkle)

NOOKS AND CRANNIES

Alyssum saxatile (Madwort)
Arabis (Rock cress)
Armeria (Thrift)
Campanula (Bellflower)
Chamaemelum nobile (Chamomile)
Erodium chamaedryoides (Heron's-bill)
Herniaria glabra (Rupturewort)
Heuchera sanguinea (Coralbells)
Iberis sempervirens (Evergreen candytuft)
Lamium maculatum (Spotted dead nettle)
Lysimachia nummularia (Moneywort)
Mentha requienii (Corsican mint)
Sagina subulata (Irish and Scotch moss)
Sedum (Stonecrop)
Sempervivum tectorum (Hen-and-chickens)
Soleirolia soleirolii (Baby's-tears)
Thymus (Thyme)

TOLERATE TRAFFIC

Ajuga (Bugleweed)
Chamaemelum nobile (Chamomile)
Dichondra micrantha (Dichondra)
Duchesnea indica (Mock strawberry)
Juniperus horizontalis 'Blue Rug' (Blue rug juniper)
Phyla nodiflora (Lippia)
Sagina subulata (Irish and Scotch moss)
Veronica repens (Speedwell)
Zoysia tenuifolia (Korean grass)

TOLERATE OCCASIONAL TRAFFIC

Achillea tomentosa (Woolly yarrow)
Arabis alpina (Rock cress)
Armeria maritima (Common thrift)
Cerastium tomentosum (Snow-in-summer)
Lysimachia nummularia (Moneywort)
Mentha requienii (Corsican mint)
Phlox subulata (Moss pink)
Potentilla (Cinquefoil)
Thymus (Thyme)
Vinca minor (Periwinkle)

AN EVERGREEN GARDEN

Allen Haskell's garden nursery in New Bedford, Massachusetts, is a testimony to a frequently forgotten garden color: green. Too often, gardeners tend to think of color only in terms of reds, blues, yellows, and oranges—the colors of seasonal annuals. But too many colors in a garden can create an unsettling mood. By using evergreen ground covers, Haskell demonstrates how well green works—by itself and as the perfect backdrop for seasonal displays.

There is a tremendous variety of evergreen ground covers available today. Most evergreens are quite hardy and, once established, require only minimal care. Consider these ground covers as the foundation of your garden. The seasonal colors come and go, but the evergreens stay beautiful the entire year.

HASKELL GARDEN NURSERY

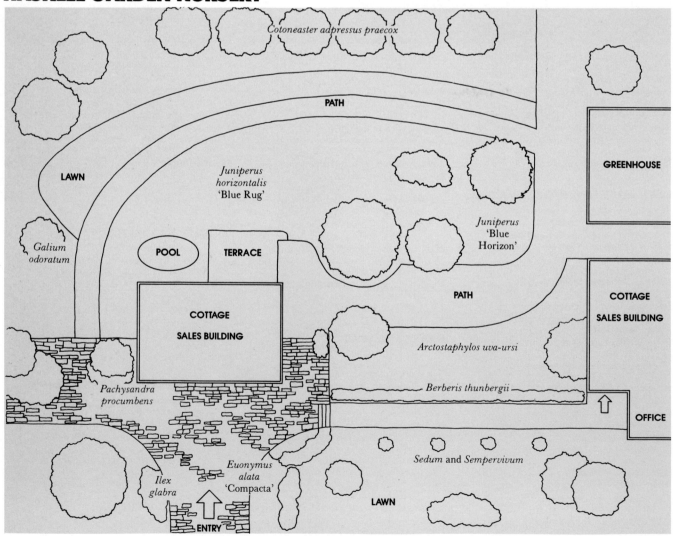

Cotoneaster adpressus praecox

PATH

LAWN

Juniperus horizontalis 'Blue Rug'

GREENHOUSE

Galium odoratum

POOL TERRACE

Juniperus 'Blue Horizon'

COTTAGE SALES BUILDING

PATH

COTTAGE SALES BUILDING

Arctostaphylos uva-ursi

OFFICE

Pachysandra procumbens

Berberis thunbergii

Ilex glabra

Euonymus alata 'Compacta'

Sedum and *Sempervivum*

LAWN

ENTRY

Above left: The entryway to the Haskell Garden Nursery features a low hedge of Japanese barberry and a bright green carpet of kinni-kinnick. The color of the full-moon maple in the background perfectly matches the crimson shade of the low barberry hedge.

Above right: Early coton-easter blends the lawn and trees into a unified landscape.

Right: The entwining foliage of 'Blue Rug' juniper creates a close-knit mat of ever-green ground cover.

Opposite page: The transi-tion from terrace to ground cover is highlighted by stone edging, specimen plants, and a barberry-sheltered bench.

Using Ground Covers Imaginatively

Have fun with ground covers. Consider a plant's potential instead of
its conventional use. Experiment with plant combinations
and growing patterns; then try your hand at bonsai or rock gardens,
topiary or hanging basket arrangements. The creative
possibilities are limited only by your imagination.

All too often, home gardeners tend to think of plants as belonging in rigid categories. Ground covers are obviously cover-the-ground plants, but they are capable of much, much more. Looking beyond a ground cover's traditional use opens your eyes to the many creative possibilities the plant provides. All it takes is the desire to do something different.

View ground covers up close and admire their variations in texture, form, color, and structure. Notice the cool, soft touch of a patch of baby's-tears; the tufting, geometric mounds of *Festuca ovina glauca*; the bright, violet flowers of *Campanula*; the serrated leaves of *Pachysandra procumbens*. Ground covers can satisfy touch, taste, smell, and sight—so give your imagination full rein in putting these versatile plants to use.

Right: Like miniature trumpets, bellflowers thrust their delicate blossoms skyward. Excellent as a hanging-basket subject.

Opposite page: Wild strawberry helps soften the lines of a garden stairway.

THINK CREATIVELY

It's fun to use ground covers in unexpected places, and your home—both inside and out—offers endless possibilities. All sorts of objects and features in your home environment can be combined with ground covers to produce displays that delight the senses.

Think containers. Small-leafed ivies make handsome hanging plants indoors. Several containers staggered at different heights can provide privacy or eliminate an unattractive view. Hang some inside and outside the same window to create a sense of depth. Let a variety of vincas tumble out of pots tucked into the drawers of an old chest or worktable. Pot some honeysuckle and hang it outdoors to create a living hummingbird feeder.

Think color. Make use of the myriad colors and color combinations of all kinds of ground covers: a yellow-tipped juniper, a silver-edged thyme, a gold-dusted ivy, a white-tinged vinca, or a gray santolina. Plant variegated varieties in a window box and let them drape in colorful contrast against the house. Create a spring bouquet of periwinkle and pansies, or mix green ground covers trailing over the front of a planter with bright yellow snapdragons or red zinnias behind them.

Think environment. Build a lath arch or trellis around a window and let honeysuckle frame your view. If you plant dwarf pyracantha in the window box below the arch, birds will come to the window for honeysuckle nectar and the bright red pyracantha berries. Honeysuckle also can help turn a gazebo into a shady, quiet retreat.

Try using ground covers to create mini-environments outdoors. Portable wall units can be made with herbs, succulents, or trailing plants. Simply make a sphagnum peat sandwich with soil as the filling (use sheets of sphagnum peat, not ground peat moss). Frame it with chicken wire and wood, insert the roots through the chicken-wire holes, and water thoroughly. After the plants are established, hang the unit outside—on a balcony railing, an outdoor wall, wherever you want to create mood or privacy. You can make a standing, modular wall unit by using heavier lumber and interplanting small-leafed ivies and bright annuals; this provides you with pretty, portable privacy.

Think whimsically. Make a living checkerboard of Scotch and Irish moss, or try designing your house number in sempervivum. Make a garden patchwork quilt combining different covers, or create a tiny Japanese garden. While you're thinking Japanese, consider bonsai. Many ground covers make outstanding bonsai subjects. Because woody ground covers, such as juniper and cotoneaster, are by nature low-growing and slow-growing, they make exceptional bonsai material. Combine a variegated juniper with gray fescue, or plant some moss beneath a cotoneaster resplendent in red winter berries.

Left: A fence is transformed into a showcase for container ivies.

Opposite top: A garden bench becomes even more inviting when bordered by lushly blooming Persian catmint.

Opposite bottom: The contrasting greens of Scotch and Irish moss are a natural for a living checkerboard.

HERB COVERS

Botanically, an herb is a nonwoody plant. In more popular usage, an herb is a plant that is valued for some culinary, cosmetic, or medicinal purpose. The latter definition permits inclusion of many nonherbaceous plants—lavender and rosemary, for example.

By either definition, many herbs slip smoothly into the role of ground covers. Herbs offer numerous assets: they display interesting textures and patterns, provide fragrance and color, and are generally easy to grow. They are sturdy and hardy with regard to temperature. The two basic horticultural requirements for most herbs are a light, well-drained soil and full sun. Limitations? Most herbs are for looking at, not walking on; they are usually too delicate or too tall for traffic. As for maintenance, while some herbs can become weedy under good garden conditions, shearing keeps them nicely under control. Landscape and cooking are improved in one simple snip.

Left: Dwarf rosemary offers aromatic foliage and is attractive spilling down a slope, wall, or the sides of a planter.

Opposite page: Training ivies over topiary forms: a 2-year-old 'Gold Heart' (left) and a 3-year-old 'California Gold'.

Below: A rock garden is a perfect location to plant a collection of ground covers. Try succulents (shown here), ferns, or flowering ground covers.

As with all ground covers, think creatively with herbs. In addition to the usual landscape uses, try small herbs in a hanging herb garden, or grow them in planters, window boxes, and in combination with other plants. Brush your hand across them to release the rich perfume of their foliage.

Following is a list of herbs that are star performers as ground covers. For details on culture and uses, see the individual listings in the "Plant Selection Guide."

Achillea tomentosa
(Woolly yarrow)

Alyssum saxatile
(Basket-of-gold)

Artemisia
(Wormwood)

Chamaemelum nobile
(Chamomile)

Galium odoratum
(Sweet woodruff)

Lavandula angustifolia
(English lavender)

Mentha requienii
(Corsican mint)

Nepeta mussinii
(Persian catmint)

Rosmarinus officinalis
'Prostratus'
(Prostrate rosemary)

Santolina chamaecyparissus
(Lavender cotton)

Stachys byzantina
(Lamb's-ears)

Teucrium chamaedrys
(Dwarf germander)

Thymus
(Thyme)

ROCK GARDENS

If you like to create formal arrangements, think about a rock garden. The contrast of rough, worn stone and the freshness of living plants is very attractive. Take a look at your yard and decide how large a garden you want. Then go rock shopping—most builders' supply houses have large, handsome specimens to choose from. After the rocks have been delivered and arranged, determine how many pockets and spaces there are and then fill them with a good, rich soil. Tamp the soil down hard—roots won't grow through air spaces—and begin choosing your plant material. Succulents are attractive and easy to grow. Or try 'Gold Dust' ivy and some hardy ferns. *Cotoneaster dammeri* spills attractively, clinging close to the rock. Select plants that provide some textural and color contrast with each other and that blend well with the rocks.

IVY TOPIARIES

Topiary is the art of living sculpture, the process of giving a plant a new and amusing shape. Small-leafed ivies make excellent topiaries when they are trained over wire forms. Shape a wire coat hanger into a circle and make a Christmas wreath, or bend some chicken wire, 1-inch fencing, or hardware cloth into a cone and create a miniature Christmas tree. With pliers, wire, and ingenuity, you can make almost any shape.

The plant-growing process is easy. Just take 4- to 6-inch cuttings of almost any ivy. Recommended cultivars include 'Hahn's', 'Maple Queen', 'California', 'California Gold', 'Gold Heart', and 'Glacier'. Strip off the lower leaves so there's at least 1 inch of stem and 1 node to insert into the rooting medium. The new roots will grow from the nodes where the leaves were. Ivy can be rooted in water, coarse sand, or a peat moss and perlite mix (use twice as much peat moss as perlite and blend thoroughly). The cuttings can be rooted in community flats or pots or simply in a glass of water. Rooting the ivy in water makes it easy to see when the roots develop; in a soil mix, wait 6 to 8 weeks and then check the rooting progress by giving each cutting a gentle tug. If there's resistance, it's rooted.

Plant rooted cuttings into 2-inch pots, 2 cuttings per pot. Any good potting soil can be used—amend packaged soil mixes with perlite or coarse sand, using twice as much packaged soil as sand. Wait 6 to 8 weeks until cuttings grow about 4 inches, then move them to 6-inch pots. Before you pot them this time, decide what kind of form you're going to use. For forms with a "trunk," pot 6 to 8 cuttings in the center of the pot. For a frame—like a cone or a pyramid—that starts at the pot's rim, plant the cuttings around the edge of the pot. You'll need 8 to 10 cuttings for the larger shapes; the idea is to get thick, full coverage of the frame.

It takes another 6 to 8 weeks before the runners are long enough (about 18 inches) to start training. Under ideal conditions it takes about 6 months from the time cuttings are taken until they are ready to start training. You can shorten this period by simply buying a 6-inch pot of a healthy, small-leafed ivy. Sometimes nurseries sell inexpensive ivies in gallon cans, and you can repot them into attractive pots. If you're using a form that starts at the rim of the pot, pinch back the cuttings 2 or 3 times to encourage branching and fullness. Once you begin to train the ivy on the topiary frame, it takes about 6 to 8 months to cover a 2-foot form, a year to cover a 3-foot form.

Animal-shaped topiaries can be made with chicken wire if the hollow "body" is stuffed with sphagnum moss. The pots of ivy can be concealed in the sphagnum inside the topiary.

Good care consists of watering thoroughly by plunging or using a narrow watering wand and then allowing the soil to dry somewhat before watering again. Ideal temperatures for small-leafed ivies are 65°F to 75°F. They winter well indoors in cold climates. Outdoors, morning sun is best; indoors, they need bright light. To keep topiaries neat and tidy, tuck in stray ends and trim topiaries lightly when they get shaggy.

Ivy topiaries are long-lived, if given good care, and delight viewers equally as much as those who create them.

Plant Selection Guide

Use this guide to acquaint yourself with more than two hundred commonly used ground covers. The plant descriptions, photographs, and culture and uses information will help you to select the ideal plants for your home landscape.

This chapter presents an encyclopedic listing of plants that are useful as ground covers. Within these pages you can find a plant for virtually every type of landscape. Although the guide is extensive, including rock garden plants, hardy perennials, and plants normally considered useful only as shrubs, it is by no means a complete listing of every ground cover plant. It reflects, instead, a wide variety of hardy, adaptable plants commonly available to home gardeners in the United States and Canada, and was compiled with the help of many writers, researchers, and growers from different climates throughout North America.

UNDERSTANDING PLANT NAMES

The "Plant Selection Guide" is alphabetical by botanical name. If you don't know or can't remember a plant's botanical name, see the guide to common names and their botanical counterparts on page 38.

There are two major types of names used to refer to plants: common names and botanical names. Although common names can be more charming and usually are easier to pronounce, there are problems with using them. One plant

Lily-of-the-valley demonstrates its beauty as a ground cover, whether viewed up close (right) or at a distance (opposite page).

Following is an alphabetical listing of ground covers by their common names. The botanical name for each plant is given in parentheses after the common name.

A

Aaron's beard *(Hypericum calycinum)*
Alpine bugle *(Ajuga genevensis)*
Alpine cinquefoil *(Potentilla cinerea)*
Alpine geranium *(Erodium chamaedryoides)*
Alpine rock cress *(Arabis alpina)*
American barrenwort *(Vancouveria hexandra)*
Andorra juniper *(Juniperus horizontalis 'Plumosa')*
Angel's hair *(Artemisia)*
Arrow broom *(Genista sagittalis)*
Asiatic jasmine *(Trachelospermum asiaticum)*
Australian violet *(Viola hederacea)*

B

Baby's-tears *(Soleirolia soleirolii)*
Baby wintercreeper *(Euonymus fortunei 'Minima')*
Barren strawberry *(Waldsteinia fragarioides)*
Barrenwort *(Epimedium)*
Basket-of-gold *(Alyssum saxatile)*
Bearberry *(Arctostaphylos uva-ursi)*
Bearberry cotoneaster *(Cotoneaster dammeri)*
Bellflower *(Campanula)*
Big Blue lilyturf *(Liriope muscari)*
Bird's-foot trefoil *(Lotus corniculatus)*
Bishop's hat *(Epimedium)*
Bishop's weed *(Aegopodium podagraria)*
Blue fescue *(Festuca ovina glauca)*
Blue leadwort *(Ceratostigma plumbaginoides)*
Blunt plantain lily *(Hosta decorata)*
Bog rosemary *(Andromeda polifolia)*
Boston ivy *(Parthenocissus tricuspidata)*
British Columbia wild ginger *(Asarum caudatum)*
Brooms *(Cytisus, Genista)*
Bugleweed *(Ajuga)*
Bunchberry *(Cornus canadensis)*
Burro's-tail *(Sedum morganianum)*

C

Canadian wild ginger *(Asarum canadense)*
Canby *(Paxistima [Pachistima])*
Carmel creeper *(Ceanothus griseus horizontalis)*
Carolina jessamine *(Gelsemium sempervirens)*
Carpet bugle *(Ajuga reptans)*
Catmint *(Nepeta mussinii)*
Caucasian wormwood *(Artemisia caucasica)*
Chamomile *(Chamaemelum nobile)*
Checkerberry *(Gaultheria)*
Chinese holly *(Ilex cornuta)*
Christmas fern *(Polystichum acrostichoides)*
Christmas heath *(Erica carnea)*
Cinquefoil *(Potentilla)*
Cliff-green *(Paxistima [Pachistima])*
Coastal wood fern *(Dryopteris arguta)*
Common aubrieta *(Aubrieta deltoidea)*
Common garden verbena *(Verbena × hybrida)*
Confederate violet *(Viola priceana)*
Coralbells *(Heuchera sanguinea)*
Corsican mint *(Mentha requienii)*
Cottage pink *(Dianthus plumarius)*
Cranberry cotoneaster *(Cotoneaster apiculatus)*
Creeping cotoneaster *(Cotoneaster adpressus)*
Creeping gardenia *(Gardenia jasminoides)*
Creeping Jennie *(Lysimachia nummularia)*
Creeping juniper *(Juniperus horizontalis)*
Creeping lilyturf *(Liriope spicata)*
Creeping mahonia *(Mahonia repens)*
Creeping speedwell *(Veronica repens)*
Creeping thyme *(Thymus serpyllum)*
Crested iris *(Iris crisata)*
Crown vetch *(Coronilla varia)*

D

Daylily *(Hemerocallis)*
Donkey's-tail *(Sedum morganianum)*
Dusty-miller *(Artemisia)*
Dwarf coyote brush *(Baccharis pilularis)*
Dwarf germander *(Teucrium chamaedrys)*
Dwarf heavenly bamboo *(Nandina domestica nana)*
Dwarf Japanese garden juniper *(Juniperus chinensis procumens 'Nana')*
Dwarf plumbago *(Ceratostigma plumbaginoides)*
Dwarf rosemary *(Rosmarinus)*

E

English holly *(Ilex aquifolium)*
English ivy *(Hedera helix)*
English lavender *(Lavandula angustifolia)*
European wild ginger *(Asarum europaeum)*
Evergreen candytuft *(Iberis sempervirens)*

F

False spirea *(Astilbe)*
Feverfew *(Chrysanthemum parthenium)*
Firethorn *(Pyracantha)*
Five-finger fern *(Adiantum pedatum)*
Five-leaf akebia *(Akebia quinata)*
Fleece flower *(Polygonum)*
Florist's fern *(Dryopteris austriaca spinulosa)*
Foamflower *(Tiarella)*
Fragrant plantain lily *(Hosta plantaginea)*
Fringed bleeding-heart *(Dicentra eximia)*
Funkia *(Hosta)*

G

Geneva bugle *(Ajuga)*
Germander *(Teucrium)*
Gold-dust *(Alyssum saxatile)*
Gold-moss stonecrop *(Sedum acre)*
Goutweed *(Aegopodium podagraria)*
Grass pink *(Dianthus plumarius)*
Green carpet *(Herniaria glabra)*

H

Hall's Japanese honeysuckle *(Lonicera japonica 'Halliana')*
Heartleaf bergenia *(Bergenia cordifolia)*
Heath *(Erica, Daboecia)*
Heather *(Calluna vulgaris)*
Hen-and-chickens *(Sempervivum tectorum)*
Heron's-bill *(Erodium chamaedryoides)*
Himalayan cotoneaster *(Cotoneaster congestus)*
Holly *(Ilex)*
Honeysuckle *(Lonicera)*
Hottentot fig *(Carpobrotus edulis)*
Hungarian speedwell *(Veronica latifolia 'Prostrata')*

I

Ice plant *(Carpobrotus)*
Indian strawberry *(Duchesnea indica)*
Irish moss *(Sagina subulata)*
Ivy *(Hedera)*

J

Japanese barberry *(Berberis thunbergii)*
Japanese holly *(Ilex crenata)*
Japanese holly fern *(Cyrtomium falcatum)*
Japanese ivy *(Hedera rhombea)*
Japanese knotweed *(Polygonum cuspidatum compactum)*
Japanese painted fern *(Athyrium georingianum)*
Japanese spurge *(Pachysandra terminalis)*
Juniper *(Juniperus)*

K

Kew wintercreeper *(Euonymus fortunei 'Kewensis')*
Kinnikinnick *(Arctostaphylos uva-ursi)*
Kirk's coprosma *(Coprosma × kirkii)*
Knotweed *(Polygonum)*
Korean grass *(Zoysia tenuifolia)*

L

Lady fern *(Athyrium filix-femina)*
Lamb's-ears *(Stachys byzantina [Stachys olympica])*
Lavender cotton *(Santolina chamaecyparissus)*
Leatherwood fern *(Dryopteris marginalis)*
Lemon thyme *(Thymus × citriodorus)*
Lily-of-the-Nile *(Agapanthus)*
Lily-of-the-valley *(Convallaria majalis)*
Lilyturf *(Liriope)*
Lingonberry *(Vaccinium)*
Lippia *(Phyla nodiflora)*

M

Madwort *(Alyssum)*
Maidenhair fern *(Adiantum pedatum)*
Maiden pink *(Dianthus deltoides)*
Manzanita *(Arctostaphylos)*
Mascarene grass *(Zoysia tenuifolia)*
Mazus *(Mazus reptans)*
Meadowsweet *(Astilbe)*
Memorial rose *(Rosa wichuraiana)*
Mirror plant *(Coprosma repens)*
Mock orange *(Pittosporum tobira)*
Mock strawberry *(Duchesnea indica)*
Mondo grass *(Ophiopogon japonicus)*
Moneywort *(Lysimachia nummularia)*
Moss phlox *(Phlox subulata)*
Moss sandwort *(Arenaria)*
Mossy stonecrop *(Sedum acre)*
Mother-of-thyme *(Thymus serpyllum)*
Mountain cranberry *(Vaccinium vitis-idaea minus)*
Mountain-lover *(Paxistima [Pachistima])*
Mountain rock cress *(Arabis alpina)*
Myrtle *(Vinca minor)*

N

Narrow-leafed plantain lily *(Hosta lancifolia)*
Natal plum *(Carissa grandiflora)*
Necklace cotoneaster *(Cotoneaster conspicuus decorus)*
Nepal ivy *(Hedera nepalensis)*
New Zealand brass buttons *(Cotula squalida)*

O

Oregon boxwood *(Paxistima myrsinites)*
Oregon grape *(Mahonia aquifolium)*

P

Parrot's-beak *(Lotus berthelotii)*
Pearlwort *(Sagina subulata)*
Periwinkle *(Vinca)*
Pernettya *(Pernettya mucronata)*
Persian ivy *(Hedera colchica)*
Peruvian verbena *(Verbena peruviana)*
Pink *(Dianthus)*
Pink clover blossom *(Polygonum capitatum)*
Pink creeping thyme *(Thymus serpyllum 'Roseus')*
Plantain lily *(Hosta)*
Point Reyes ceanothus *(Ceanothus gloriosus)*
Pork and beans *(Sedum × rubrotinctum)*
Prostrate myoporum *(Myoporum parvifolium)*
Prostrate rosemary *(Rosmarinus officinalis 'Prostratus')*
Purpleleaf wintercreeper *(Euonymus fortunei 'Colorata')*
Pyrenees cotoneaster *(Cotoneaster congestus)*

R

Red-osier dogwood *(Cornus sericea)*
Ribbon grass *(Phalaris arundinacea 'Picta')*
Rock cotoneaster *(Cotoneaster microphyllus)*
Rock cress *(Arabis)*
Rock rose *(Cistus)*
Rockspray cotoneaster *(Cotoneaster microphylla)*
Rose *(Rosa)*
Rupturewort *(Herniaria glabra)*

S

Sageleaf rock rose *(Cistus salviifolius)*
Sand strawberry *(Fragaria chiloensis)*
Sandy pink *(Dianthus arenarius)*
San Jose juniper *(Juniperus chinensis 'San Jose')*
Savin juniper *(Juniperus sabina)*
Scotch heather *(Calluna vulgaris)*
Scotch moss *(Sagina subulata 'Aurea')*
Scotch pink *(Dianthus plumarius)*
Sea fig *(Carpobrotus edulis)*
Sea pink *(Armeria maritima)*
Serbian bellflower *(Campanula poscharskyana)*
Shield fern *(Polystichum)*
Shore juniper *(Juniperus conferta)*
Siberian tea *(Bergenia crassifolia)*
Silky-leaf woadwaxen *(Genista pilosa)*
Small Himalayan sarcococca *(Sarcococca hookeriana humilis)*
Small-leafed cotoneaster *(Cotoneaster microphyllus)*
Snow-in-summer *(Cerastium tomentosum)*
Speedwell *(Veronica)*
Spotted dead nettle *(Lamium maculatum)*
Sprenger asparagus fern *(Asparagus densiflorus 'Sprengerii')*
Spring cinquefoil *(Potentilla verna)*
Spring heath *(Erica carnea)*
Squaw carpet *(Ceanothus prostratus)*
St.-John's-wort *(Hypericum calycinum)*
Star jasmine *(Trachelospermum jasminoides)*
Stonecress *(Aubrieta)*
Stonecrop *(Sedum)*
Sun rose *(Helianthemum nummularium)*
Sweet alyssum *(Lobularia maritima)*
Sweet woodruff *(Galium odoratum)*

T

Thrift *(Armeria maritima)*
Thyme *(Thymus)*
Trailing lantana *(Lantana montevidensis [Lantana selloviana])*
Trailing verbena *(Verbena peruviana)*
True Scotch heather *(Calluna vulgaris)*

V

Variegated goutweed *(Aegopodium podagraria 'Variegatum')*
Variegated wintercreeper *(Euonymus fortunei 'Gracilis')*
Violet *(Viola)*
Virginia creeper *(Parthenocissus cinquefolia)*

W

Wall rock cress *(Arabis caucasica)*
Wavy-leafed plantain lily *(Hosta undulata)*
Western sword fern *(Polystichum munitum)*
Whisky nose *(Sedum × rubrotinctum)*
White Chinese indigo *(Indigofera incarnata 'Alba')*
White creeping thyme *(Thymus serpyllum 'Alba')*
Wild ginger *(Asarum)*
Wild strawberry *(Fragaria)*
Wilton carpet juniper *(Juniperus horizontalis 'Wiltonii')*
Wintercreeper *(Euonymus)*
Wintergreen *(Gaultheria procumbens)*
Woodbine *(Parthenocissus cinquefolia)*
Wood fern *(Dryopteris)*
Woolly speedwell *(Veronica incana)*
Woolly thyme *(Thymus pseudolanuginosus [Thymus lanuginosus])*
Woolly yarrow *(Achillea tomentosa)*
Wormwood *(Artemisia)*
Wrinkleleaf rock rose *(Cistus crispus)*

Y

Yaupon *(Ilex vomitoria)*
Yellow archangel *(Lamium galeobdolon)*

can have many different common names, varying from region to region, even person to person. Or a particular common name in one part of the country may refer to an entirely different plant in another.

Since anyone can (and they do!) make up new common names for plants at whim, some standardization of names is necessary to avoid confusion. The International Code of Nomenclature for Cultivated Plants is the worldwide authority for horticultural names. The code insures that every plant has one, and only one, correct identification: the botanical name. Always in Latin, this name is divided into two parts. The *genus* is analogous to a human surname, indicating a general group of plants with many similar botanical characteristics. For example, *Juniperus* is the generic name for a juniper. The *species* is a more specific category within a genus and forms the second part of a plant's name: *Juniperus chinensis* is a specific juniper, the Chinese juniper.

A *variety* is a further subdivision of a species and is distinguished by a plant's ability to pass on its identifying traits through its seed. Varieties occur in the wild. Varietal names are indicated in Latin and follow the species name: *Juniperus chinensis sargentii* is the sargent juniper.

A *cultivar* is similar to a variety, except that it is the product of deliberate horticultural development. Cultivar names follow either the species or variety name and in this book are capitalized and set off by single quotation marks—for example, *Juniperus chinensis* 'San Jose', the San Jose juniper.

Finally, the term "varieties" is used in a larger sense to refer to a group of plants that includes both botanical varieties and cultivars.

USING THE PLANT SELECTION GUIDE

The plant descriptions in the following guide detail the distinguishing features and best ways to grow, propagate, and make use of each ground cover. (To help you select plants for special situations, also see the landscaping lists on pages 26 and 27.) Since it is not possible to predict definitively how a plant will adapt to every particular climate, site, and set of growing conditions, keep in mind that such terms as "fast-growing" or "drought-tolerant" are relative. A plant that grows unmanageably in one location, for example, may be quite well behaved in another.

Glancing through the "Plant Selection Guide" will give you an introduction to the variety of ground covers available. If a photo or reference to a particular plant captures your attention, you can read about the plant in detail in its individual listing. Or simply read the guide from start to finish to become intimately acquainted with the wealth of ground covers from which you can choose.

Nursery shopping: Doing your gardening homework will make it easier to select a ground cover.

Achillea
(Woolly Yarrow)

Woolly yarrow *(Achillea tomentosa)* is a sturdy, low-maintenance, evergreen herb with narrow, soft, feathery, gray green leaves 1 to 4 inches long. Its growth habit is spreading and rapid. Tight clumps form a dense, matlike cover 8 to 12 inches high. From spring through summer, 2- to 3-inch-wide, flat clusters of tiny, yellow blossoms appear at the top of 4- to 10-inch stems.

Culture: Woolly yarrow requires full sun and a well-drained soil. It is fairly drought-tolerant and needs only moderate watering during the summer. Propagate by seeds or division. Set out rooted transplants 6 to 12 inches apart, preferably in spring. Trim off old flower stalks periodically to help maintain continued flower production. Cut stems back to the ground in fall, at the end of the blooming period. Hardy to −45°F.

Uses: Woolly yarrow is commonly used in rock gardens and as a border plant. Mowed lightly, it may be used as a lawn substitute where foot traffic is light. It provides erosion control on moderate slopes.

Adiantum
(Five-finger Fern, Maidenhair Fern)

Adiantum pedatum is a hardy maidenhair fern. This beautiful, fine-textured ground cover has 5 frondlets on each of its dark,

wiry stems. The delicate, airy fronds grow up to 2 feet tall. The plant spreads by means of creeping rootstalks.

Culture: Five-finger fern thrives in shade to partial sun and soil rich in humus. Keep the soil moist and apply a leaf mold mulch to prevent the delicate, fibrous roots from drying out. Hardy to −40°F.

Uses: This fern adapts well as an understory ground cover and looks lovely in the shade of trees and shrubs. It may be interplanted with flowers or tucked into the pockets of a stone wall.

Aegopodium
(Goutweed, Bishop's Weed)

Goutweed *(Aegopodium podagraria)* is a hardy, fast-growing, deciduous perennial. The leaves are blue green and usually edged with white. Goutweed forms a low, dense mat up to 6 inches high. Clusters of tiny, white flowers (resembling Queen Anne's lace) on stems 12 to 18 inches high appear in June. The flowers produce seeds that germinate wherever they fall to the ground. Goutweed is very vigorous and apt to become a weed if not controlled. Variegated goutweed *(A. p.* 'Variegatum') is somewhat less vigorous and the most widely planted form.

Culture: Goutweed grows in either sun or shade, but growth is slower in the shade, making it more manageable. It

Adiantum pedatum

tolerates poor soil and dry conditions. Propagate by seeds or division. Even a small piece of the creeping roots can start a new plant. Hardy to −35°F.

Uses: Goutweed may be mass-planted, but management is easiest when it is planted between barriers, such as a sidewalk and a house foundation. Mowing 2 or 3 times a season keeps it low and even, and the leaves small and compact.

Agapanthus
(Lily-of-the-Nile)

Agapanthus is a summer-flowering perennial with leathery, straplike leaves and fleshy roots. There are both evergreen and deciduous varieties varying in size and flower color.

Agapanthus orientalis is most commonly cultivated. Its leaves are evergreen, about 2 feet long and 2 inches wide. Flower stalks (to 4 or 5 feet) bear large, spherical clusters of tubular flowers in shades of white and blue.

A. africanus is a smaller version of *A. orientalis*. Leaves are narrow (½ inch) and flower stalks reach to 1½ feet.

A. inapertus is deciduous, with dark blue flowers that hang from 4- to 5-foot

Achillea tomentosa

Aegopodium podagraria 'Variegatum'

The ajuga used most commonly as a ground cover is carpet bugle *(A. reptans)*. It's fast-growing and spreads by creeping stems. Foliage consists of tight clusters of somewhat oval, wavy leaves 2 to 4 inches long that form a thick, low mat. For a short time in the spring, flower spikes rise 4 to 6 inches above the foliage. The many cultivars of carpet bugle include:

'Atropurpurea': bronze leaves and blue flowers.

'Giant Bronze': larger and more vigorous; metallic bronze leaves.

'Giant Green': same as above but with bright, crisp green leaves.

'Jungle Green': larger, more rounded leaves of crisp green; flower spikes 8 to 10 inches.

'Jungle Bronze': slightly smaller leaves are more rounded; growth is more rounded.

'Rubra': dark, purplish leaves.

'Variegata': leaves edged and mottled with pale yellow.

Culture: The ajugas grow best in partial sun to light shade. The deeper the shade, the larger and more succulent the leaves grow. Ajugas need a well-drained soil or else stem and root rot diseases are likely to develop. Propagate by division; plant in spring or fall, spacing divisions 6 to 12 inches apart. Water moderately, more in full sun—plants should not be allowed to dry out. In cold-winter areas some protection from winter winds is advised. Plants are rejuvenated by mowing lightly after blooming. Hardy to −10°F.

Uses: Carpet bugle is particularly effective when planted in the semishade of other plants or buildings. Along a path it provides a cool, rather formal effect. Flowers are a short-term bonus; the plant's landscape value is based on its handsome foliage.

flower stalks. Leaves are 2 inches wide and 2½ feet long.

'Dwarf White' agapanthus is evergreen, 1½ feet tall, and bears white flowers on 2-foot stalks.

'Peter Pan' is evergreen also and very dwarf (8 to 12 inches tall). Blue or white flowers are clustered at the top of 15-inch stalks.

Culture: Lily-of-the-Nile is an adaptable plant. It thrives in full sun but grows well in partial shade, although it won't flower as profusely. Lily-of-the-Nile grows best in good garden soil but tolerates heavy soil. Ample water is recommended, especially when the plants are in bloom. Remove flower stalks after they've finished flowering. Divide clumps every 5 or 6 years. Lily-of-the-Nile is easy to grow in mild-winter climates. Hardy to 15°F.

Uses: The evergreen types make good ground covers when mass-planted, providing a dramatic display when in bloom. As an accent, use them in clumps around rocks or combine with English ivy or dwarf vinca.

Ajuga
(Bugleweed, Ajuga)

The ajugas are hardy perennials, long favored by gardeners for their ease of

cultivation, fast growth, and showy flower spikes. There are three species.

The Geneva or alpine bugle *(Ajuga genevensis)* is more a rock garden plant than a ground cover. It has no runners and grows in a matlike clump. Flowers are blue, rose, or white.

A. pyramidalis is another clump-forming type having no runners. Leaves are clear green and large; flowers are violet. The cultivar 'Metallica Crispa' has metallic, reddish brown leaves with crisp edges.

Ajuga reptans

Akebia
(Five-leaf Akebia, Akebia)

Five-leaf akebia *(Akebia quinata)* is a gracefully twining, semi-evergreen vine. It's a vigorous grower (up to 15 feet each year), especially in mild climates, and has few insect or disease problems. The deep green leaves are divided into 5 leaflets and are borne on 3- to 5-inch stalks. The plant is evergreen in mild climates, and the foliage remains on the plant late into the season in colder areas. Rosy purple flowers appear in the spring, and purple, fleshy, edible pods may develop.

Culture: This plant grows in sun or shade, prefers a well-drained soil, and requires moderate watering. Propagate by seeds, cuttings, or root division. Hardy to −30°F.

Uses: Five-leaf akebia is a highly adaptable plant. It can be useful on slopes or open areas, where its billowy foliage quickly covers bare ground and its deep roots hold the soil, providing some erosion control. It should be planted away from low-growing shrubs since its aggressive habit can smother them.

Alyssum
(Basket-of-gold, Gold-dust, Madwort)

Alyssum saxatile (also known as *Aurinia saxatilis*) is an herbaceous perennial. This classic rock garden plant is best known for its bright golden-yellow flower clusters that appear in the spring. The plant grows to about 6 inches and the grayish green leaves are 2 to 5 inches long.

Akebia quinata

Alyssum saxatile

Culture: Basket-of-gold thrives in full sun and a well-drained soil. Keep it on the dry side. The plant is easily raised from seed but is taprooted, so it should be transplanted while still young. Basket-of-gold self-sows freely once established in the garden. Stimulate compact growth by cutting back stems after flowering. Plant 10 to 12 inches apart. Hardy to −30°F.

Uses: Plant basket-of-gold in a prominent spot in the front of a garden or along a border to show off its brilliant color. It also can be grown in containers and moved to suitable spots in the landscape.

Andromeda
(Bog Rosemary)

Andromeda polifolia is an evergreen shrub that grows in boglike conditions. Bog rosemary has leathery leaves about 1½ inches long and reaches a height of about 1 foot. In April or May, clusters of tiny, china pink flowers appear at the branch tips. Bog rosemary spreads by under-ground rootstock. Cultivars available include 'Nana' and 'Montana', which are lower and more compact.

Culture: Andromeda prefers full sun but will tolerate some shade. It requires wet, acidic soil and grows easily wherever cranberries thrive. Propagate by layering or cutting sections of the creeping roots. Hardy to −50°F.

Uses: Bog rosemary is best used in wet, acidic soils—the types of soil in which most plants cannot survive. Reserve bog rosemary for these spots.

Arabis
(Rock Cress)

Usually rock cresses are used as border and rock garden plants. They flower in shades of white or pink in spring or summer, and they are easy to grow. Two varieties make good small-space ground covers.

Alpine or mountain rock cress *(Arabis alpina)* bears leaves that are evergreen and smooth. The plant grows to

Andromeda polifolia

Arabis caucasica

10 inches. In the spring, fragrant, white flowers are borne in such profusion that foliage is completely hidden below them.

Wall rock cress *(A. caucasica)* is the more common type. In fact, plants sold as *A. alpina* are often *A. caucasica*. Wall rock cress may be distinguished by the fine, feltlike, whitish hairs that give the leaves a grayish cast. The flowers are profuse and fragrant.

Culture: Rock cress requires full sun and lots of heat to thrive. The soil should be well-drained. Once established, very little water is needed; the plants are drought-tolerant. After flowering, cut back the upright stems to induce horizontal growth. One plant will cover a square foot. Propagate by seeds, cuttings, or division. Alpine rock cress is hardy to −35°F, and wall rock cress is hardy to −5°F.

Uses: These are not large-scale ground covers but are perfect nook-and-cranny plants. They are especially suited for covering slopes, spilling over walls, and tucking between stones. They combine well with aubrieta, *Phlox subulata*, and *Alyssum saxatile*. Try rock cress in containers too.

Arctostaphylos
(Bearberry, Kinnikinnick, Manzanita)

Most species of *Arctostaphylos* are shrubs or small trees. A few species are low-growing and make attractive ground covers. One of the best for this purpose is *A. uva-ursi*, which grows around the world in northern latitudes. It is a sturdy, evergreen, drought-resistant, slow-growing plant that grows 6 to 10 inches high. Branches, which can spread to 15 feet, are covered with oval, leathery, bright green leaves up to 1 inch long that turn red where winters are cold. In the spring, bell-shaped, white or light pink flowers appear at branch ends. Two handsome cultivars are 'Point Reyes', characterized by darker green leaves set more closely together on shiny red stems, and 'Radiant', notable for a heavy crop of bright red berries that appear in fall and last most of the winter.

A few other *Arctostaphylos* species are useful as ground covers, although they are less commonly available than *A. uva-ursi*. One is *A. edmundsii*, a mild-climate California native that is more heat- and drought-resistant than *A. uva-ursi*. Among all manzanita ground covers, *A. edmundsii* 'Carmel Sur' is the fastest-growing, forming a dense, 8- to 10-inch-high ground cover.

Culture: *A. uva-ursi* and its cultivars need full sun in mild-summer areas and partial shade in hot-summer areas. Bearberry requires a well-drained soil. To look attractive in a home garden, it needs summer watering once every 4 to 6 weeks in loose, fast-draining soil, less in heavy soil. Propagate by seeds, cuttings, or division. In spring, set out rooted plants 6 inches or less apart to reduce weed growth. Except for pruning out dead areas, plants should be left untouched. Hardy to −40°F to −50°F.

Uses: Bearberry is effective as a large-scale planting in informal or native gardens, particularly on slopes or trailing over a wall.

Arctostaphylos uva-ursi

Arctostaphylos edmundsii 'Little Sur'

Armeria maritima

Arenaria
(Moss Sandwort)

Arenaria verna (caespitosa) is a mosslike, evergreen, perennial herb. It is sometimes mistakenly called Irish moss (see *Sagina subulata*). Moss sandwort has small, narrow, dark green leaves that form a dense, slowly spreading, 3-inch mat. Tiny, white flowers appear in the summer.

Culture: Moss sandwort prefers partial shade but tolerates full sun. It grows in well-drained soil and needs regular watering, with the amount of water increased the more it is exposed to full sun. It is best propagated by dividing plants in the spring. Hardy to −50°F but needs some winter protection in cold, exposed locations.

Uses: Moss sandwort is best used as accent clumps bordering a wall or planted between steppingstones or in a rock garden. It tolerates light foot traffic.

Armeria
(Thrift, Sea Pink)

Thrift *(Armeria maritima)* is a sturdy, evergreen perennial that grows in dense, grassy clumps. It blooms in the spring, into summer in inland areas, and even longer in coastal and cooler areas. The delicate pink or white flowers are borne on long, thin stems. Height can range from 2-inch tufts and 3- to 5-inch flower stalks, to 10-inch tufts with flowers rising above 2 feet. Clumps spread slowly to about 15 inches.

The appearance of thrift varies, depending upon soil conditions, exposure, and variety. Because of the number of varieties and natural hybridization, you cannot always be certain from names given to young plants just precisely what you may end up with. Common varieties are *alba* (white flowers), *californica* (shorter stems, larger flowers), and *purpurea* (purple flowers). There are many others.

Culture: Thrift thrives in medium shade or full sun and a well-drained soil and requires only moderate watering during hot summer months. To insure accurate reproduction, plants are best propagated by division. Hardy to −50°F.

Uses: Thrift is used typically in rock gardens and as a border or edging plant. It's very useful because of its general toughness, long blooming period, delicacy of flowers, and interesting leaf texture. When kept low, it becomes ideal for use between steppingstones.

Artemisia
(Dusty-miller, Wormwood, Angel's Hair, Artemisia)

Artemisias are sturdier-than-they-look, perennial herbs characterized by lacy, silver gray, finely cut foliage. They produce tiny, inconspicuous, yellow flower heads for a short time at summer's end.

Caucasian wormwood *(Artemisia caucasica)* is sold at some nurseries under the name 'Silver Spreader'. It forms a dense mat 3 to 6 inches high that spreads 2 feet or more. The foliage of fringed wormwood is whiter and is carried on the upper part of 12- to 18-inch stems that are woody at the base. *A. schmidtiana* forms dense, tufted mounds; two cultivars differing only in height are 'Silver Mound', about 1 foot tall, and 'Nana', a few inches tall.

Arenaria verna

Asarum europaeum

Culture: These plants thrive in full sun but tolerate partial shade. They need a well-drained soil. Artemisias are drought-tolerant and require only moderate watering. Tall varieties should be cut back as they become rangy. Propagation by seeds is slow; it's better to divide them. Plant artemisias in the spring, placing low varieties 6 inches apart and taller varieties 12 inches apart. Hardy to −25°F.

Uses: Artemisias are accent plants, typically effective as borders in places where their soft, pale color and interesting leaf pattern contrast with brightly colored plants. They tolerate light foot traffic.

Asarum
(Wild Ginger)

The wild gingers are incomparable ground covers for the heavily shaded, woodland soils to which they are native. Although not related to culinary ginger, the creeping rootstalks and pungent leaves have a gingerlike fragrance. The 2- to 7-inch, heart-shaped leaves are borne on 7- to 10-inch stalks. Reddish brown flowers are below the foliage, so are usually not noticed, and appear in early spring. There are several species.

Asarum caudatum (British Columbia wild ginger) is evergreen and probably most commonly available. It's native to the coastal mountains of the western United States and British Columbia. *A. europaeum* (European wild ginger) is almost identical to *A. caudatum* except for its shinier, glossier leaves. Both are hardy to −25°F. Other evergreens are *A. arifolium* and *A. virginicum.* They are similar except for reduced cold tolerance (to −15°F). They are native to the southeastern United States.

Deciduous types are native over much of the eastern United States. *A. canadense* (Canadian wild ginger) can be used as a ginger substitute by collecting and drying the creeping roots. It's one of the most hardy, tolerating temperatures to −35°F. *A. shuttleworthii* is similar but has thinner, mottled, usually larger leaves and is hardy to −15°F. Deciduous forms are not cultivated as frequently as evergreen ones because of the lack of winter effect.

Culture: The gingers are native to woodlands where shade is heavy and the soil is high in humus and moisture. With lots of water, gingers can grow in heavy soils low in organic matter, but they do best in soils that are either naturally high in humus or generously amended. Locations protected from drying winds are best. Propagate by dividing the creeping rootstalks.

Uses: In a naturalistic woodland garden, gingers form an exceptionally attractive, dense mat. Combine them with evergreen shrubs or wildflowers.

Asparagus
(Sprenger Asparagus Fern)

Sprenger asparagus (*Asparagus densiflorus* 'Sprengeri') is one of several species of ornamental asparagus admired for their fernlike foliage. Often used as a container plant, its trailing growth habit and arching sprays of light green, needlelike leaves make it useful as a ground cover in mild climates. Clusters of tiny, pinkish white flowers appear in spring and early summer, followed by equally small, bright red berries that soon drop off. The growth rate is moderate and the plant can be expected to billow up to about 18 inches.

Culture: Sprenger asparagus grows well in full sun or light shade. It grows well in any good garden soil. This is a sturdy, drought-resistant plant that requires little care but looks best with regular watering and occasional feeding. Propagation is easy by seeds or division. As a ground cover it is restricted to warm-winter areas. Hardy to 25°F.

Uses: Sprenger asparagus is best used in small areas. It is effective in a raised bed, where it might be designed to cascade over a low wall. It has small prickles and a natural tendency to cling to, or climb, other plants. For this reason, it is best grown alone.

Artemisia schmidtiana 'Silver Mound'

Asparagus densiflorus 'Sprengeri'

Athyrium filix-femina

Astilbe
(False Spirea, Meadowsweet, Astilbe)

Astilbes are long-lived perennials that add a dramatic accent as a small-scale ground cover. The delicate flowers that appear in the spring are the main attraction. A few of the many cultivars and colors available include: 'Bridal Veil', pure white; 'Cattleya', pink; 'Diamond', white; 'Deutschland', creamy white; 'Fanal', deep garnet-red; 'Peach Blossom', pale peach-pink; and 'Rheinland', carmine pink.

Culture: Astilbes thrive in shade or partial sun; they need some shading from intense light. They grow best in a cool, well-drained soil that is rich in humus and need to be kept moist. For best flower display, astilbes should be divided every 3 or 4 years and fertilized each spring. Cut them back after flowering. Roots are shallow, so deep-working the soil is not necessary, but a mulch is. Good soil drainage is especially important because astilbes are very sensitive to water-logged conditions in winter. (Plant in mounds or raised beds to improve drainage.) In some areas Japanese beetles are a pest. Control them with an insecticide containing carbaryl.

Uses: Astilbes are attractive near pools and streams and in woodland settings. They combine well with hostas and bergenias and adapt to container culture.

Athyrium
(Lady Fern, Japanese Painted Fern)

Athyriums are delicate, deciduous, 2- to 4-foot ferns. They are very easy to grow.

The most common species is the lady fern *(Athyrium filix-femina)*. It tolerates more sun and less moisture than most ferns and spreads thickly enough to out-compete most weeds. It is shaped like a vase and has yellow green fronds. For collectors, there are many named varieties.

The Japanese painted fern is *A. goeringianum*. The cultivar 'Pictum' is

Astilbe

lower—to 1½ feet—and has slightly drooping fronds, notable for their coloring. The ruby red stems and main veins contrast strikingly with the soft, gray green fronds.

Culture: These are hardy plants that grow just about anywhere. As with most ferns, ideal conditions include partial sun to shade, good garden soil, and lots of moisture. Protection from wind is advised or the fronds will become ragged looking.

Uses: The lady fern makes an excellent ground cover in woodland gardens or along streams. The unusual coloring of the Japanese painted fern makes it an interesting accent plant—use it where it can be appreciated at close range.

Aubrieta
(Common Aubrieta, Stonecress)

Aubrieta deltoidea is a common rock garden plant that grows in a low, spreading manner. Usually it grows between 2 and 6 inches tall and spreads 1 to 1½ feet. The leaves are a warm gray color. The plant blooms in the spring, producing ¾-inch flowers that range in color from light rose to deep purple.

Aubrieta deltoidea

Culture: Aubrieta thrives in full sun (light shade in hot-summer areas) and a well-drained soil with moderate watering. It can be killed by overwatering in the winter or lack of watering in the summer. Shear plants back halfway after the flowers die and before the seeds set. Periodic application of an all-purpose fertilizer is beneficial. Aubrietas are easily grown from seeds: sow in late spring for flowers the following spring. You also can divide plants after they bloom in the spring or take cuttings in the fall. Hardy to −20° F.

Uses: Aubrieta is commonly used in rock gardens and for edging. Often it is planted with *Phlox subulata, Alyssum saxatile,* and *Iberis sempervirens.* Aubrieta does particularly well in the Northwest and is a commonly used plant in that region.

Baccharis pilularis 'Twin Peaks'

Baccharis
(Dwarf Coyote Brush)

Dwarf coyote brush (*Baccharis pilularis*) is an evergreen shrub that makes an excellent ground cover. It is available primarily in the western United States, where it is native. Leaves are small, lightly toothed, dark green, and closely set on woody branches. The shrub grows at a moderate rate to about 2 feet (sometimes higher with age) and spreads 3 to 8 feet. Inconspicuous flowers appear at the leaf ends in summer. The cultivar 'Twin Peaks' is similar but has a lower, more compact growth habit. It has been the most commonly used form. The less well-known cultivar 'Pigeon Point' is greener, grows faster, and is higher and more mounding. It spreads to at least 10 feet.

Culture: These are remarkably adaptable plants, growing equally well in sun or shade and in almost any type of soil. They are known for their drought tolerance but also tolerate wet conditions. Propagate by cuttings, spacing the rooted plants 1½ to 3 feet apart in the fall; cover the area with a mulch to inhibit weeds. Dead wood and arching branches should be pruned out each spring.

Uses: These tough, green plants grow inland or at the beach and provide superior erosion control. For high-desert gardens, baccharis is one of the most reliable ground covers. It has been widely used as a bank cover and is very handsome draping over walls.

Berberis
(Japanese Barberry)

Japanese barberry (*Berberis thunbergii*) is a deciduous, 4- to 8-foot-high shrub with bright red berries, spiny arching branches, and brilliant yellow to scarlet autumn foliage. Many of its cultivars have a low or compact growth habit and are suitable for use as ground covers. The most popular, and one of the best, is 'Crimson Pygmy' (often sold as 'Atropurpurea Nana'). It forms a compact mound about 1 foot high and 2 feet across. The foliage consists of blood red leaves, ½ to 1 inch long, set densely along the branches. The leaves retain their color through spring and summer.

Culture: Japanese barberry grows well in sun or partial shade, but red-leafed forms such as 'Crimson Pygmy' need full sun for the best color to develop. These plants are tolerant of all kinds of soil and need only moderate watering; they are very drought-tolerant. The capacity to withstand neglect and extremes of climate and soil is, perhaps, their most outstanding quality. Propagate by seeds, layering, or softwood cuttings. Hardy to −20° F.

Uses: The low-growing or compact cultivars of *B. thunbergii* are excellent ground covers for gentle slopes, along paths, and in dry, rocky areas. The spiny branches discourage traffic.

Berberis thunbergii 'Crimson Pygmy'

Bergenia cordifolia

Bergenia crassifolia

Bergenia
(Heartleaf Bergenia, Siberian Tea)

These common perennials are often not appreciated for the dramatic accents they can provide. The leaves are large and leathery, and handsome pink, white, or rose flower spikes appear in the spring. Two species are well known.

The heartleaf bergenia (*Bergenia cordifolia*) grows to 20 inches high. The leaves are fleshy, grow to 10 inches long, have wavy edges, and are heart-shaped at their base, where they connect to the stem. The flower spikes are 15 inches tall.

Siberian tea (*B. crassifolia*) is quite similar to *B. cordifolia*, but the leaves are shorter by 2 or 3 inches, are finely toothed, and do not have a heart-shaped base. Flower spikes are taller by 3 or 4 inches and emerge in winter in mild-climate areas.

Culture: Plant bergenias in some shade, protected from wind that can tear the large leaves (in cool, coastal areas, full sun is fine). Bergenias grow best in a well-drained soil that is kept moist. Cut the plants back when the thick, woody rhizome becomes leggy; if clumps become crowded, divide them. Water and fertilize regularly and bait for snails and slugs. Hardy to −45°F.

Uses: Bergenias are commonly used for shady borders, in clumps among smaller-leafed ground covers, around irregular surfaces such as rocks, and by pools and streams. They combine well with ferns, hostas, and tall rhododendrons.

Calluna
(Scotch Heather)

Calluna is one of three genera (*Erica* and *Daboecia* are the others) that comprise the heaths and heathers. The many varieties of Scotch heather (*C. vulgaris*) are somewhat hardier than the heaths (to −20°F) and have smaller, overlapping, evergreen leaves that are suggestive of junipers. They also grow taller—some varieties reach 2 feet. Different leaf colors are available, ranging from yellow gold to the familiar light green. The minute, bell-shaped flowers are about ¼ inch long and are available in many shades of red and white.

Culture: The requirements of *C. vulgaris* are the same as those of heaths (see *Erica* for details). Heathers are somewhat slower-growing than heaths, however, so plants should be spaced closer to one another—about 1 foot apart. Use a mulch to control weeds until the cover is established.

Uses: The low-growing heathers are useful as borders and edging plants as well as ground covers. Their deep roots help prevent soil erosion on steep slopes. Heathers can withstand salt-laden air and exposed, windy locations and are therefore well suited to coastal locations. Like heaths, they require very little mainte-nance once established.

Campanula
(Bellflower)

The nearly 300 species of *Campanula* are characterized by mostly bell-shaped flowers in various shades of blue. 'Adriatic bellflower' (*C. elatines garganica*), usually sold as *C. garganica*, is the lowest-growing. It forms a loose, 3- to 6-inch-high mat of heart-shaped, green leaves, 1½ inches wide, that grow at the end of spreading stems. The plant blooms from late summer into fall, producing many

Calluna vulgaris

violet blue, star-shaped (rather than bell-shaped) flowers. Serbian bellflower (*C. poscharskyana*) is similar but taller, reaching up to 1 foot in height. Its flowers, also star-shaped, display a more lavender hue. It has a trailing growth habit, spreading rapidly by creeping runners.

Culture: In cold climates and coastal areas these plants grow best in full sun; in warmer climates they need light shade. Bellflowers are sturdy plants that grow well in almost any soil with good drainage. In dry-summer areas they require watering 2 or 3 times a month. Propagate by seeds or by dividing plants in the spring, spacing plants about 10 inches apart. Bellflowers can be invasive and should be contained or separated from other plants by a header or divider. Hardy to −40°F.

Uses: Adriatic bellflower and Serbian bellflower are best for small-scale planting; both need to be seen up close to be appreciated. Adriatic bellflower is attractive under the filtered shade of a large tree, such as a sycamore, where it can nudge up against exposed roots. It also is effective spilling over a stone wall. Serbian bellflower is lovely as an accent plant in any shaded garden area.

Lampranthus

Campanula poscharskyana

Carpobrotus, Delosperma, Lampranthus
(Ice Plant, Sea Fig, Hottentot Fig)

There are many different "ice plants" — trailing, spreading, or bushey. All are sturdy, almost maintenance-free, colorful, and drought resistant.

The sea or hottentot fig (*Carpobrotus edulis*) is one of the most widely used ground covers along the coastal freeways between San Diego and San Francisco. The daisylike flowers vary from pale yellow to deep pink. The plants have a trailing growth habit, succulent leaves, and edible figlike fruits in the fall.

White trailing ice plant (*Delosperma* 'Alba') is fast growing and widely available. An almost continuous bloom of small white flowers provides a color contrast with the attractive green leaves.

Lampranthus species are the most common, showy, brilliantly colored of all the ice plants. They range from 10 to 15 inches in height and produce masses of daisylike flowers.

The orange-yellow, bushy *Lampranthus aurantiacus* has predominantly orange flowers. The variety 'Sunman' has yellow-orange, and 'Glaucus' has yellow flowers. They bloom from late February into May with a scattering of flowers through summer.

The purple spreading ice plant, *L. productus*, spreads from 18 to 24 inches and blooms from January through April — about a month earlier than other species. Flowers are purple and 1 inch wide.

Trailing ice plant (*L. spectabilis*) is highly visible in spring (March through May) when it produces masses of flowers that cover the foliage. Trailing ice plants are available in pink, rose-pink, red, and purple. Flowers are about 2 inches across and plants are 6 to 12 inches high.

Culture: Ice plants do best in porous soil and full sun. They are propagated by cuttings or divisions spaced 12 to 18 inches apart. In arid climates, water two or three times during the dry season to keep plants in top condition.

Uses: Best described as eye-catchers, ice plants are dramatically effective in mass plantings covering level ground or slopes. They are also excellent for erosion control on steep slopes.

with narrow, woolly leaves ¾ inch long. The foliage is covered with ½-inch, white flowers from spring into summer. Snow-in-summer spreads about 2 feet each year; ultimately, a single plant can cover 9 square feet.

Culture: For optimum appearance, the plant needs full sun and a well-drained soil. It is drought-resistant but looks better with a weekly watering in hot, dry-summer areas. Propagation is easy by seeds, division, or cuttings. Set plants 1 to 2 feet apart in the spring. A planting can be mowed lightly at the end of its blooming period to remove dead flower heads. Hardy to −40°F.

Uses: Snow-in-summer is best used for large- or small-scale planting wherever its unusual color can contrast well with its surroundings. It may be used effectively on slopes or level ground, or between steppingstones.

Ceratostigma
(Dwarf Plumbago, Blue Leadwort)

Ceratostigma plumbaginoides is an easy-to-grow, wiry-stemmed perennial. It is valued for its long-lasting, ½-inch flowers, which appear in late summer and last until fall. It grows in tufts up to 12 inches tall and spreads rapidly by underground stems. The leaves are dark green, about 3 inches long, and develop a reddish tint in the fall. In the mildest climates some leaves remain throughout the winter, but most usually die to the ground; new growth appears by late spring.

Ceanothus
(Wild Lilac, Redroot)

Several low-growing species of wild lilac make beautiful ground covers. These evergreen shrubs are native to the western United States and are available mainly in that area. These plants are not related to true lilacs but get their common name from their lilaclike blossoms.

Point Reyes ceanothus (*Ceanothus gloriosus*) forms a dense, evergreen mat 1 to 1½ feet high, spreading slowly to about 5 feet. The leaves are leathery, dark green, 1½ inches long, and mostly round. The plant blooms in late spring, producing clusters of violet blue flowers.

Carmel creeper (*C. griseus horizontalis*) forms a dense cover 1½ to 2½ feet high and spreads 5 to 15 feet. It produces violet blue flower clusters 2 to 3 inches long. A more compact cultivar, 'Compacta', grows only 1 foot high.

Squaw carpet (*C. prostratus*) is the lowest-growing ceanothus, forming a dense mat about 3 inches high that spreads to 10 feet wide. It has the typical leathery, small, roughly edged, dark green leaves and small, rounded clusters of blue flowers.

Culture: Wild lilacs need a sunny location and a light, well-drained soil.

Good drainage is important; the plants do not tolerate wet conditions. In a home garden they can develop root rot from receiving more summer waterings than they would in the wild. Two deep waterings a month in hot-summer areas are plenty after the plants are established. Ceanothus are difficult to propagate by seeds and cuttings. It is best to buy the plants from nurseries, where it is possible to check the numerous varieties available. Hardy to 0°F.

Uses: These plants are excellent for seaside gardens, where they are almost maintenance-free. With attention to watering needs, they can be grown successfully inland. They make fine accent plants in informal settings.

Cerastium
(Snow-in-summer)

Snow-in-summer (*Cerastium tomentosum*) is a popular evergreen ground cover because of its striking, light gray foliage, its toughness, and its adaptability to almost any growing condition. It forms a dense mat 4 to 6 inches high. Masses of slender stems spread along the ground and then turn upward; their upper sections are covered

Cerastium tomentosum

Ceratostigma plumbaginoides

Chamaemelum nobile

Culture: Dwarf plumbago takes full sun or light shade. Many soil types are tolerated as long as drainage is good. Supply moderate amounts of water; more if the plants are growing in full sun. Cut plants back in the fall, after the flowers have died. Propagate by division in the spring; space the plants 1 to 2 feet apart. Hardy to −10°F.

Uses: Dwarf plumbago is an adaptable plant with many possible uses. It can cover fairly large areas and is attractive tucked into corners or under shrubs. It combines well with English boxwood, ajuga, or sempervivums.

Chamaemelum
(Chamomile)

Chamomile (*Chamaemelum nobile*, formerly known as *Anthemis nobilis*) is an evergreen, perennial herb long popular in Europe as a lawn substitute. It's also famous for chamomile tea, made from dried flower heads. During summer, small greenish or yellowish flower heads with white petals appear at the top of slender stalks. Chamomile has lacy, dramatic, lustrous, grass green leaves that form a soft mat 3 to 12 inches high. It spreads at a moderate rate.

Culture: Chamomile grows best in light, sandy soil in full sun and tolerates some shade. Its deep roots make the plant drought-resistant, and it requires only moderate watering in summer. Chamomile is easily propagated by division in spring or fall; set new plants 6 to 12 inches apart. Hardy to 0°F.

Uses: Left to grow to its natural height, chamomile is an adaptive plant in small areas of the garden. Sheared, it is attractive between steppingstones. Mowed and rolled, it can serve as a lawn substitute or a living, growing path, made more attractive by the pleasant fragrance it gives off when walked upon. If you like herb teas, the dried flower heads of chamomile make one of the finest. Steep them in hot (not boiling) water for 10 to 15 minutes. The herb only lightly colors the water—judge strength by smelling. Traditionally, chamomile is a relaxing bedtime drink. Legend has it that it is the only known cure for nightmares.

Chrysanthemum
(Feverfew)

Feverfew (*Chrysanthemum parthenium*) can grow in a crack in a driveway and persist even after it presumably has been ripped out. It is a leafy, upright ornamental with great numbers of small (¼- to ½-inch), white daisy flowers that bloom throughout the summer. It grows 2 to 3 feet high. Cultivars include 'Golden Ball', yellow flowers; 'Silver Ball', double-flower forms in white; and 'Golden Feather', chartreuse foliage, 8 to 10 inches high.

Culture: Feverfew self-sows freely or, like the cultivars, can be propagated by division. The cultivars also can be propagated by seeds. These plants can be sheared occasionally to keep them low and more compact. Hardy to −10°F.

Uses: Feverfews are used chiefly as fillers or for contrast among other bedding plants. At one time, tea made from the flower heads was taken medicinally to reduce fever; hence its popular name.

Chrysanthemum parthenium 'Golden Ball'

Cistus
(Rock Rose)

The rock roses are fast-growing, evergreen, mostly upright shrubs distinguished by lovely, roselike flowers. Two species are low-growing and can be planted as ground cover.

The sageleaf rock rose (*Cistus salviifolius*, often erroneously called *C. villosus* 'Prostratus') has delicate, white flowers with yellow spots at the base of the petals. The flowers appear in profusion from late spring into midsummer. The leaves are gray green, rather small, oval, and sparsely hairy. Mature shrubs reach 2 feet in height and spread to about 6 feet.

Wrinkleleaf rock rose (*C. crispus*), relatively new to the nursery trade, is a distinctly prostrate, rigidly branched species, growing to a maximum height of 18 inches. It has deep green foliage with wavy leaves that are slightly aromatic when crushed. Flowers are a striking red-pink with a bright yellow center. They are the same size as those of *C. salviifolius* (1 to 1½ inches wide) and have the same blooming period.

Culture: Rock roses are sun-loving plants that perform best in a coarse, well-drained soil. They are extremely drought-tolerant and are resistant to insect pests and disease. Established plants require little or no summer water where the climate is moderated by the ocean. Some irrigation may be needed, however, in hot interior valleys and in the desert. Maintenance requirements for *C. crispus* are minimal; *C. salviifolius* tends to be a little rank, so tip pruning is desirable to keep the plant compact and to encourage prostrate growth. Though the species are sturdy, withstanding drying winds, heat, and salt spray, they are not reliably hardy below about 15°F.

Uses: Both *C. crispus* and *C. salviifolius* are excellent large-scale

Convallaria majalis

ground covers for steep slopes and for areas where irrigation and maintenance cannot be provided. They have deep, extensive root systems for controlling soil erosion. These species are also valuable for landscaping to reduce fire hazards around homes in brush areas. Finally,

they are effective in rock gardens and as informal borders where there is no traffic.

Convallaria
(Lily-of-the-valley)

Lily-of-the-valley (*Convallaria majalis*) is one of the hardiest and most adaptable ground covers. It thrives in partial or full shade and develops a dense mass of soil-holding roots. Leaves die back in the fall and are renewed in spring. New leaves grow to 8 inches long and 1 to 3 inches wide. The fragrant, ¼-inch, usually white, bell-shaped flowers appear in spring. Available cultivars include 'Fortins Giant', which has larger flowers, and 'Rosea', with pale pink flowers.

Culture: Lilies-of-the-valley are undemanding and grow in just about any soil. Planted on 7-inch centers, they spread to create a ground cover that needs almost no attention. Periodic feeding

Cistus

Coprosma repens

improves them. Divide the clumps anytime. Divisions, called pips, can be planted to increase your own supply or to share with neighbors. Hardy to −40°F, though the plants do not thrive or bloom well in climates that do not provide freezing winters.

Uses: Lilies-of-the-valley are deciduous, best where the lack of winter foliage won't be missed. They are used typically around shrubs, such as the taller rhododendrons and camellias, and also are effective with ferns.

Coprosma
(Coprosma)

Kirk's coprosma (*Coprosma × kirkii*) is a sturdy, evergreen shrub composed of woody, upright, heavily branched stems lined with yellow green, oblong leaves ³⁄₄ inch long. The growth rate is moderate to 1½ to 2½ feet.

The mirror plant (*C. repens*) is a shrub that can reach 6 feet wide and 10 feet high but is extremely pliable and easily kept to any desired height by pruning 2 or 3 times a year. Its leaves are 3 inches long and the greenish white flowers are barely noticeable. Several variegated forms are available.

Culture: These coprosmas grow in sun or partial shade and in almost any soil. They are drought-resistant and need only light summer watering. Hardy to 20°F.

Uses: Coprosmas are useful in an informal setting planted against a fence or, pruned to develop compact growth, as a low hedge. Their best use might be as a small-scale ground cover on a slope near the beach, where they can withstand wind and spray.

Cornus
(Bunchberry, Red-osier Dogwood)

There are two relatives of the well-known dogwood tree that are useful as ground covers: bunchberry (*Cornus canadensis*) and red-osier dogwood (*C. sericea*).

The bunchberry is native from Alaska to New Mexico to West Virginia, always growing in cool, moist, acidic soil. In open woodlands it can be found covering areas up to a mile square. It spreads (not invasively) by underground runners and rarely grows taller than 9 inches. Tiny flower clusters appear in early spring and are surrounded by white bracts that look just like the "flowers" on their larger relatives. Bright red fruits mature by late summer, then turn yellow to red in the fall.

The red-osier dogwood is a deciduous, spreading shrub that grows to 5 to 7 feet in height. It is appreciated for its winter color of bright red twigs. Pruning the branches to the ground every 3 or 4 years produces more brightly colored twigs. The cultivar 'Kelseyi' is a dwarf form that rarely exceeds 2 feet and 'Flaviramea' has yellow twigs.

Culture: Bunchberries have an undeserved reputation for being difficult to establish. For the best chance of success, don't skimp on soil preparation. The soil should be loose and acidic with much leaf mold, pine needles, or peat worked in; transplant whole sods (if possible) in 5- or 6-square-foot sections. Plant in a site that is cool and moist but has plenty of springtime sun (such as under deciduous trees).

Uses: Once established, these are plants of rare beauty. Bunchberry does well in woodland and mountain gardens and as a ground cover around rhododendrons and similar plants. The red-osier dogwood is coarse and taller-growing but does spread and become quite dense. Because of the periodic pruning that is needed, use it in small, manageable clumps. This plant's best use is on banks and in wet soils.

Cornus canadensis (left and right)

Coronilla
(Crown Vetch)

The deep, soil-building roots and dense, weed-choking, 2-foot top growth of crown vetch (*Coronilla varia*) have made this one of the most popular ground covers for erosion control. The highway departments between Illinois and Pennsylvania have used it extensively. It dies back in winter, and the mass of brown stems can be a fire hazard in some areas. Leaves consist of many ½-inch, oval leaflets. Pinkish flowers appear in summer.

Culture: Crown vetch can be planted by seed, using about 1 pound per 1,000 square feet. Transplanting crowns (on 2-foot centers) or whole sods are more reliable ways to establish a cover. Once established, fertilizer is not particularly needed. Crown vetch is drought-resistant; it prefers full sun but tolerates some shade. It spreads by underground runners, so it can be invasive and difficult to eradicate. If possible, mow in the spring (using a sharp rotary or flail-type mower), and it will make a beautiful green summer carpet. Hardy to −40°F.

Uses: Crown vetch is excellent for erosion control and for large, difficult-to-maintain areas. Honeybees use the flowers and cattle eat the foliage.

Cotoneaster
(Cotoneaster)

There are many cotoneasters suitable as ground covers. Among them are varieties adapted to virtually every climate of North America. They are deep-rooted and good soil binders, each variety producing attractive flowers in spring and berries in fall.

Creeping cotoneaster (*Cotoneaster adpressus*) is a deciduous type that eventually reaches 1 foot high and spreads 6 feet. Small, ¼-inch flowers are pink-tinted; red fruits are the same size. Leaves are small (½ inch) and dark green. Early cotoneaster (*C. a. praecox*) is more vigorous and slightly larger. It becomes taller (to 1½ feet) and has slightly larger leaves and berries. Creeping cotoneaster is noted for its short, rigid branches and dense, low habit. Hardy to −20°F.

Cranberry cotoneaster (*C. apiculatus*) is very similar to the more common rock cotoneaster. It differs mainly by its larger berries that remain on the plant throughout winter. It is deciduous, grows to 1 to 2 feet high, and spreads to 4 or 5 feet. Flowers are pinkish and appear in clusters; leaves are nearly round, usually less than ½ inch in diameter, and slightly hairy on the undersides. Hardy to −20°F.

The Himalayan or Pyrenees cotoneaster (*C. congestus*) is evergreen. It is slow-growing to about 3 feet and spreads 3 feet in 5 years. Flowers are small, whitish pink, and appear in June. Berries are bright red. Leaves are similar to the rockspray cotoneaster but more rounded and without the fine hairs. The Himalayan cotoneaster is one of the hardy evergreens. Because of its slow growth rate, it is easy to care for once established. Hardy to −5°F.

The necklace cotoneaster (*C. conspicuus decorus*) is an extremely prostrate evergreen form. Secondary branches grow vertically to 1 to 1½ feet. Ultimate spread is 6 to 8 feet. Flowers are white and berries are fairly large, covering the branches in fall. Leaves are ¼ inch long and are dark green on top with paler undersides. Necklace cotoneaster is a good ground cover but is not dense enough to shade out weeds. It is best used in containers or rock gardens. Hardy to 0°F.

Bearberry cotoneaster (*C. dammeri*) is distinct on two counts: it's the flattest of the cotoneasters, spreading only 10 feet and only becoming ½ to 1 foot tall, and it's the hardiest of the evergreen cotoneaster ground covers, tolerating temperatures to −10°F. Flowers are white and the masses of bright red fruits are highly ornamental. Leaves are 1 inch long and oval-shaped, glossy green above, and pale, sometimes whitish beneath. There are two cultivars. 'Lowfast' is a very fast-growing ground cover, possessing slightly smaller leaves more widely spaced on the branches. 'Skogsholmen', a Swedish cultivar, is similarly vigorous and fast-growing but is also noted for its spring-time flower display. These are handsome but uneven woody plants, neat all year and fine for close-up viewing; they are some of the very best for following surface contours or cascading over walls.

The rock cotoneaster (*C. horizontalis*) is perhaps the most widely grown of all. It's semi-evergreen in mild climates, losing leaves for only a short time; elsewhere it's deciduous but so heavily covered with bright red berries that leaves aren't missed. Mass plantings maintain a 3- to 4-foot height. Branches eventually spread to 8 to 10 feet, sometimes more. Flowers and fruit are small; leaves are round, ½ inch in diameter, and become reddish in color before falling. Rock cotoneaster is good in combination with low-growing junipers. It's heavily textured and especially effective on banks and in low dividers to discourage traffic. Hardy to −20°F.

The smallest-leafed, finest-textured type is the rockspray or small-leafed cotoneaster (*C. microphyllus*), an evergreen that spreads trailing branches to 6 feet; smaller branches grow upright to 2 or 3 feet. White flowers appear in June; scarlet red berries mature in the fall. Leaves are small, ¼ to ½ inch long, and shiny green on top. Fine hairs give the undersides of the leaves a grayish cast.

There are three varieties of the rockspray species. 'Cochleatus' is a more dwarf form. You can recognize it by the broad-at-the-tip, spoon-shaped leaves. The leaf edges are sometimes rolled upward. It is an interesting plant often used as a bonsai. *Thymifolius* is a very compact form and has stiff, upright branches. It's small enough for the rock garden. 'Emerald Spray' is resistant to fireblight, a disease that sometimes attacks cotoneasters.

The tangled, intermingling stems of rockspray are well suited for banks or around rocks. This cotoneaster must be

thriving to look good and benefits from soil amendments before planting. It is a popular variety in the South. Hardy to −10°F.

Culture: Cotoneasters are tough and hardy plants. They're easy to grow, transplant, and care for, thriving in heavy clay soil.

Some pests can be damaging to cotoneasters. Watch out for scale, red spiders, and lace bugs (see the chart on page 19). Fireblight, a bacterial disease, also attacks cotoneasters. Leaves suddenly wilt on an infected twig, turn brown, but don't fall off. Spray flowers every 4 to 5

days with bordeaux, fixed copper, or streptomycin spray. When pruning dead branches, cut at least 4 inches into apparently healthy wood; the disease is present beyond the damaged area. To avoid spreading the disease, burn diseased wood and disinfect pruning tools after use with a 5 percent bleach solution.

Very little pruning of cotoneasters is necessary, but occasionally dead or awkward branches need to be removed. Otherwise, prune only to encourage the graceful arching of the branches. Don't use hedge shears—the resulting stubbed branches are unattractive.

Cotoneaster dammeri '**Lowfast**'

Dichondra micrantha

Dichondra
(Dichondra)

Dichondra micrantha (formerly known as *D. repens*) is a prostrate, herbaceous perennial that comes as close to duplicating the ornamental functions of grass as any lawn substitute can—in those areas where it can be grown. Dichondra turf is formed by masses of dark green, cupped, horseshoe-shaped leaves that are ¼ to ¾ inch across. They grow atop delicate stems averaging 1 to 3 inches in height. The plant spreads at a moderate rate by surface runners that develop roots.

Culture: Dichondra grows in sun or light shade and in heavy or light soil. The important consideration is that the soil be kept evenly moist but never soggy. In hot, dry areas and in fast-draining soil, daily watering is needed; in cool, humid areas and in heavy soil, less frequent watering will suffice. Dichondra is commonly grown from seeds or by plugs. It is also widely available in a sod form, enabling you to have an instant lawn. In all cases, the soil must be prepared as carefully as for a grass lawn. Seeds sown at the rate of 1 pound per 1,000 square feet will establish a lawn in about 2 months. A flat of dichondra cut into 3-inch-square plugs will provide fast or slow cover depending on how far apart the plugs are spaced.

As with fine grass lawns, dichondra requires regular fertilizing during the active growing season. Water well after fertilizing to avoid burning the leaves. A weed killer is needed for a newly planted lawn and, later, to control invading grasses such as Bermuda grass and crabgrass. Dichondra is not hardy, although it might survive brief exposure to 15°F. Don't walk on frozen dichondra; your footprints will remain as dead spots.

Uses: Where the use of water for lawn irrigation is not a problem, dichondra makes a beautiful lawn substitute—to some, more attractive than grass. Its chief advantage over grass is that it rarely needs to be mowed. Its limitations are that it takes only the lightest traffic and is not really rugged enough for use between widely spaced steppingstones. It is also less resistant to weed invasion than most grasses.

Dryopteris
(Wood Fern, Shield Fern)

Dryopteris is a large group of ferns that includes many natives of forests in the United States and Canada. Most are very hardy, evergreen, and easy to grow.

The florist's fern is *D. austriaca spinulosa*. It is widely distributed throughout eastern North America. Its fronds are harvested in summer and shipped in winter. Hardy to −35°F.

A good landscape accent plant also native to the Northeast is the leather wood fern (*D. marginalis*). It grows in clumps to about 2 feet and is hardy to −35°F.

The coastal wood fern (*D. arguta*) is native to western North America. It grows to about 3 feet and is hardy to 0°F.

Culture: All wood ferns need shade and a moist, humus-rich soil. Many forms spread by underground runners and thus are easily propagated by division.

Uses: These are special-purpose ground covers, not used to cover large areas but to accent or complete a landscape. They are best in natural or native gardens.

Duchesnea
(Indian Strawberry, Mock Strawberry)

Indian strawberry (*Duchesnea indica*) has a superficial resemblance to *Fragaria chiloensis* but differs in several significant, but identifying respects. Its leaves are thinner and smaller and its flowers are yellow. It forms an equally dense, but somewhat lower mat and spreads rapidly by runners like the wild strawberry.

Culture: The cultural requirements are the same as for *F. chiloensis* with one important difference: it does best in light shade. It is also much hardier, to −30°F.

Dryopteris marginalis

Duchesnea indica

Uses: Indian strawberry is most attractive as a mass planting among a small grouping of trees or, in smaller areas, in the filtered shade of shrubs.

Epimedium
(Barrenwort, Bishop's-hat)

The epimediums are easy to grow, hardy, and too little used. They spread with creeping roots to make a uniform, 9-inch-high soil cover. The plant is semi-evergreen; most of the leathery, heart-shaped leaves die back in winter, but a few last into January. In early spring the new leaves are a pale green with some rose color. During midseason they are a deep, glossy green, and in fall they are reddish. Tiny, ½-inch, orchidlike flowers (shaped like a bishop's hat) appear in May. Many colors are available, and the flowers last well when cut.

Epimedium grandiflorum is the most commonly cultivated form. It grows to about 1 foot. Different cultivars offer different flower colors. 'Rose Queen' has bright, rose-colored flowers with spurs tipped white. The hybrid *E. × versicolor* 'Sulphureum' has yellow flowers. *E. × youngianum* 'Niveum' grows compactly and has white flowers.

Culture: These are long-lived, easy-to-grow perennials. Light shade is usually best, but full sun is all right if the soil (acidic is best) is rich and moist. The creeping roots are close to the surface, so don't cultivate around them. Placed 10 inches apart, the plants will fill in without overcrowding. To propagate, divide the clumps in early spring. Cut off old leaves so that small flowers and new leaves will be visible. Epimediums are very hardy, tolerating temperatures to −40°F.

Uses: Epimediums thrive in the light shade of other acid-soil plants such as the taller rhododendrons, camellias, and ferns. Their roots compete well with tree roots, so plant them around trees such as crabapple and magnolia.

Epimedium × youngianum 'Niveum' (left and right)

 *—see caption above*

Erica
(Heath)

Heaths are special plants loved by many collectors. Enough varieties are available so that mild-climate landscapes can bloom all year. These plants are finely textured and, when in flower, are covered by small, red to white, bell-shaped flowers.

Erica carnea is called either spring or Christmas heath. In mild-winter areas it begins blooming as early as November. More severe winters hold it in check until spring. This plant makes an excellent ground cover, requiring little care once established. It is low, rarely exceeding 1 foot, and spreads to 2 or 3 feet (plant on 2½-foot centers). The evergreen leaves are less than ¼ inch long and circle the stem in groups of 4. Flowers hang and are 1 to 2 inches long. In cold climates some winter protection may be necessary. Spring heath prefers acidic soil but does tolerate slight alkalinity. The best flowering is attainable in full sun, but in hot-summer areas afternoon shade is advisable. Hardy to −10°F. *E. vagans* (Cornish heath) is bushy and rounded in most varieties and is noted for its color and hardiness.

Other plants are included in the general category of heaths. The *Daboecia* genus is composed of evergreen, heathlike shrubs that are grown and used in much the same manner as *Erica. D. cantabrica* (Irish heath) is an 18-inch shrub that carries slightly drooping, ½-inch flowers on upright stems. Blooming begins from February to May, continues throughout summer, and lasts as late as November. The leaves are most similar to *Calluna* (Scotch heather) but are smaller. Several different flower colors are available. The species is lavender; the cultivar 'Alba' is white, and 'Praegerae' is rose pink. Propagate by cuttings or division. Hardy to −10°F.

Culture: Heaths are tough, low-maintenance plants. Soil must be acidic, moist, and especially well drained. If soils are too dry or water-logged, add generous amounts of organic matter. Planting in raised beds or mounds also improves drainage. Heaths stay more compact and flower better in soils that are not too rich. Roots are close to the surface, so instead of using a cultivator, apply a mulch to keep the soil loose. In early spring, cut back to remove flower stalks and to stimulate dense growth. By pinning a branch to the ground and mounding soil over it (layering), you can easily increase your supply of these plants.

Uses: The low-growing heaths serve very well not only as ground covers but also as borders and edging plants. Deep and tightly woven roots help prevent soil erosion on banks and slopes. These plants tolerate salt-laden coastal air and exposed, windy locations. The flowers dry and last many months indoors. Heaths are excellent low-maintenance ground covers, requiring almost no attention once established.

Erodium
(Heron's-bill, Alpine Geranium)

Erodium chamaedryoides is notable for its dense, delicately textured, green foliage that grows in clumps 3 to 6 inches high, spreads to about 1 foot in one season, and turns reddish in winter. Leaves are small, lightly lobed, and ovate. White, pink-veined, ½-inch-wide flowers bloom from spring through summer. The cultivar *E. c.* 'Roseum' has pink flowers veined with red. The plant's growth rate is moderate. It gets its popular name heron's-bill from the ½-inch-long, needlelike stalks seen at the stem ends after the flowers fall off.

Erica vagans

Culture: Erodium is a tolerant, adaptable plant but prefers shade, a soil with good drainage, and enough water to keep it on the moist side. It is easily propagated by seeds or division; set plants 6 inches apart for quick coverage. Hardy to 20°F.

Uses: Erodium is excellent in rock gardens and as a small-scale ground cover. It takes no traffic.

Euonymus
(Wintercreeper)

The wintercreeper (*Euonymus fortunei*) is an evergreen vine or shrub that makes a very useful ground cover where it is given nothing to climb and allowed to grow flat. Pointed, somewhat leathery, dark green, jagged leaves, 1½ to 2 inches long, are set opposite one another along trailing stems that often root where they touch moist soil. Flowers are only occasionally produced and are inconspicuous. The plant spreads rapidly to about 4 feet while building up to a height of about 2 feet.

Several cultivars make better ground covers than the species. The most widely used is purpleleaf wintercreeper (*E. f.* 'Colorata'), characterized by the striking color of its foliage in fall and winter, when it turns various hues of purple. It forms a fairly dense carpet 6 to 10 inches high.

'Kew' (*E. f.* 'Kewensis') and baby wintercreeper (*E. f.* 'Minima') are dwarf types that are more delicate, slower- and lower-growing, reaching a height of hardly more than 2 inches. Both retain their small, evergreen leaves throughout the year, the leaves of 'Minima' being somewhat larger. Variegated wintercreeper (*E. f.* 'Gracilis') is smaller, less vigorous than 'Colorata', and is notable for its variegated, whitish leaves that take on a pink tinge in winter. The virtues of *E. f. radicans* are that it is the fastest-growing of the small-leafed varieties and has leaves that are uniform in size and shape.

Culture: Wintercreepers are hardy, sturdy plants that grow in most parts of the country, in sun or shade, and in good or poor soil. They are drought-resistant but do not do well in hot, desert areas even when adequately watered. 'Colorata' tends to get tall but responds well to mowing at an 8-inch height. Wintercreepers can be propagated by division, layering, or cuttings. Divided or rooted plants should be planted in spring and set about 2 feet apart. Euonymus are particularly subject to scale infestation. Euonymus scale first causes yellowish or whitish spots on the leaves; later, leaves drop and branches die. Control scale with a dormant oil spray in early spring,

followed by Orthene or diazinon sprays when the orange red crawlers appear. Hardy to −20°F.

Uses: The dwarf and other small-leafed varieties are not good for large-scale planting but are highly effective trailing over walls and between rocks and stepping-stones. *E. f.* 'Colorata' is excellent for mass planting, particularly on steep hillsides, where it provides good erosion control, or wherever it might serve to cover barren, unsightly places.

Festuca
(Blue Fescue)

Blue fescue *(Festuca ovina glauca)* is an attractive ornamental grass composed of hairlike leaves growing 4 to 10 inches high in rounded, bluish gray tufts. Although a true grass, it is not a practical lawn substitute because of its mounding habit.

Culture: Blue fescue is successfully grown in ordinary, well-drained soil and full sun. It is drought-resistant but does need regular summer watering. Weeding between tufts can be minimized by the application of a light mulch. Shabby plants can be clipped to remove seed heads, restore appearance, and to stimulate new growth. Start new plants from divisions. Blue fescue is hardy everywhere, tolerating temperatures to −40°F.

Uses: When planted in a fairly large area, blue fescue looks best in geometric patterns rather than at random. Two or three plants can provide an effective accent; a row of plants makes a good walk border or edging for a flower bed.

Festuca ovina glauca

Fragaria chiloensis

Galium odoratum

Fragaria
(Wild Strawberry, Sand Strawberry)

A parent of all commercial strawberries, the evergreen *Fragaria chiloensis* forms a highly attractive, thick mat of 2-inch, dark green leaves that turn a reddish hue in winter. The leaves are oval, roughly toothed on their upper parts, crinkly textured, and glossy. A profusion of white, 1-inch-wide flowers appears in spring, followed by small, edible, but not too tasty fruit. A hybrid known as Hybrid Ornamental Strawberry Number 25, developed and tested in southern California, is similar, but it grows more vigorously, is larger in all respects, and produces delicious fruit.

Culture: Wild strawberry grows in full sun and in most well-drained soils; it does particularly well in sand dunes at the beach. Regular watering is needed throughout the year. Foliage growth is stimulated by light mowing in the spring. New plants are best started from sections of runners planted 12 inches apart. Wild strawberry is subject to infestations of red spider, which can be controlled by spraying twice a year with a combination spray. Hardy to −15°F.

Uses: Wild strawberry is excellent anywhere in the garden, in beds or as borders, contributing a delightful, woodsy effect. It is an ideal ground cover at the beach, particularly on slopes. It also accepts light traffic.

Gardenia jasminoides 'Prostrata'

Galium
(Sweet Woodruff)

Sweet woodruff (*Galium odoratum*) is a beautiful ground cover for shady spots. It grows rapidly, spreading by underground stems to become a dense, high mat. Tiny, white flowers in the shape of 4-petal crosses last from April into summer. They appear in clusters at the end of slender stems, 6 to 12 inches high, that are covered by long, narrow leaves set in whorls of 8. The leaves have a delicate fragrance suggestive of fresh hay or vanilla.

Culture: This is one perennial herb that does best in partial or full shade and moist, loamy soil. It is most easily propagated by dividing the creeping stems at the beginning of the dormant winter period. In spring, set out new plants 8 to 12 inches apart. Sweet woodruff self-sows freely once established. Hardy to −30°F.

Uses: This plant provides a lovely effect under trees, well-developed rose bushes, rhododendrons, and along garden paths. It gives a feeling of shady forest and

Gazania 'Sunburst'

is also a good bulb cover. Dried leaves are used in sachets, as a tea, and to flavor wine drinks, including May wine. Sweet woodruff is too delicate for traffic.

Gardenia
(Creeping Gardenia)

Gardenia jasminoides 'Prostrata' is often sold as *G. radicans*. It is a low- and slow-growing, evergreen form of the common gardenia. Ultimately, it becomes 12 inches high and spreads 2 to 3 feet. The fragrant, white flowers appear in early summer and are about 1 inch in diameter. Glossy, dark green leaves are often streaked with white. Hardy to 15°F.

Culture: Like the common gardenia, this plant prefers a moist, acidic, well-drained soil. Frequent replenishing of an organic mulch and high summer heat are necessary for success with creeping gardenia. Full sun is acceptable, but some shade is preferred. Prune upright-growing branches to stimulate horizontal growth. If sooty mold (caused by whiteflies) becomes a problem, spray with Orthene.

Uses: Creeping gardenia is an excellent small-scale ground cover and a good container plant. The miniature flower makes a perfect boutonniere.

Gazania
(Gazania)

This perennial ground cover is widely used in California and the Southwest. Gazania flowers come in a variety of colors including white, pink, yellow and brown. All bloom from late spring through summer and intermittently the rest of the time. Foliage is typically grayish, fairly dense, and reaches a height of 2½ to 6 inches.

The variety 'Sun Gold' is deep yellow at the center, lighter yellow at the tips; 'Sun Burst' has the same gradation in Orange.

Culture: Gazanias grow satisfactorily in moist soils that have good drainage. They must have a warm, sunny location, and two or three waterings a month in hot weather. They are easily propagated by dividing plants in the spring.

Uses: Gazanias are effective as specimen plants and in mass plantings. They are also effective on slopes and in parking and median strips as borders.

Gelsemium
(Carolina Jessamine)

Popular in gardens as far north as Virginia, *Gelsemium sempervirens* has escaped cultivation in many areas. Usually the plant is evergreen, but it loses its shiny green, finely textured leaves in winter in cold climates. It is most appreciated for its fragrant flowers—the state flower of South Carolina—which are yellow, tubular, and about 1 inch long and appear in early spring.

Culture: This plant tolerates some shade but flowers more profusely in full sun. Prune selectively and frequently to keep it low (about 3 feet) and to encourage new growth from the base. Almost any soil is suitable, but the plant grows best in good loam. Propagate by seeds or cuttings. The plant isn't bothered by pests. Hardy to about 15°F.

Uses: Carolina jessamine is generally best used to cover large areas. It looks attractive on a bank or spilling over a retaining wall.

Gelsemium sempervirens

Genista
(Broom)

This group of shrubs is so closely related to cytisus that the two are difficult to distinguish. Genista, like cytisus, is an excellent plant for poor and dry soils, adapted to dry-summer Mediterranean climates. One of the best ground cover species is *Genista pilosa*, which has the interesting common name of silky-leaf woadwaxen. Leaves are about ½ inch long and deciduous. In winter the bare twigs remain green. The plant spreads (forming a clump) to 7 feet wide and 1 foot or more high, though usually lower. Yellow, pealike flowers appear in May. Hardy to −10°F.

The arrow broom (*G. sagittalis*) is one of the most hardy brooms, tolerating temperatures to −20°F. Its branches are bright green in winter, and it flowers in June. Its height and spread are roughly the same as for *G. pilosa*.

Culture: Like cytisus, these are plants for hot, dry, sunny situations. They are exceptionally tolerant once established but can be difficult to transplant. Propagate by cuttings taken in August. See *Cytisus* for more information.

Uses: These are good rock garden and low-maintenance plants that blend quietly into the landscape most of the year except for springtime, when their flowers become eye-catchers.

Hedera
(Ivy)

Ivy (*Hedera*) makes an ideal ground cover: it stays green all year; spreads rapidly while staying low to the ground; climbs, covers slopes, and prevents erosion; succeeds in full sun or heavy

Genista pilosa

Hedera helix 'Gold Heart'

shade and in most climates; and is easy to propagate.

There are five species of ivy, of which *H. helix* (English ivy) and *H. canariensis* (Algerian ivy) are the most commonly used in the United States. The other species are *H. colchica* (Persian ivy), *H. nepalensis* (Nepal ivy), and *H. rhombea* (Japanese ivy).

H. helix has dark green leaves, mostly 3- to 5-lobed, that are generally 2 to 4 inches long. The plants trail and root as they spread, creating a ground cover 6 to 8 inches high. English ivy has the largest number of cultivars, primarily because of ivy's *sporting* tendencies— spontaneous changes in a plant's genetic makeup that result, for example, in leaves that may differ from the original in color, size, shape, or arrangement. *H. h.* 'Hibernica' is perhaps the most familiar and useful ground cover ivy. *H. h.* 'Baltica' ranks with 'Hibernica' in usefulness and is one of the hardiest ivies; its leaves are smaller (1 to 2 inches long), slightly darker green, and have more prominent veins than those of 'Hibernica'. Other cultivars include 'Deltoidea' (dull, dark green, heart-shaped leaves with gray

green veins), 'Green Feather' (compact-growing, with bird's-foot-shaped leaves), and the many variegateds, including 'Herold', 'Gold Heart', and 'Sulphurea'.

H. canariensis has shiny green, 3- to 5-lobed leaves up to 8 inches across, although most foliage is about half this size. This plant also roots as it spreads along the ground. Algerian ivy is more aggressive than English ivy and requires more moisture. It also has a coarser texture and looks best at a distance. Because it is tougher than English ivy and better adapted to sunny locations, it is frequently used as a freeway ground cover in areas where it is adapted. Among its cultivars, *H. c.* 'Variegata' has leaves that are edged in a yellowish white color.

Culture: It is easy to grow ivies with great success if the plants' cultural needs are observed. It is best to begin a bed with established plants purchased from a nursery. Space young English ivy plants 12 inches apart, Algerian ivy 18 inches apart. Ivies require a well-drained soil and, contrary to popular belief, high light intensity. They grow best in indirect light but, once established, tolerate full sun (if kept well watered) or even fairly heavy shade. Although ivy can survive in deep shade, it does not thrive there.

After the initial growth—ivy spurts in spring and, particularly, in fall—you can take cuttings. Ivies root easily, even in water. It's best to make 2-node cuttings and place them in a well-moistened flat of propagating soil. Cuttings should be set shallowly in the soil; the deeper you stick them into the propagating medium, the more likely they are to rot. Provide indirect light until roots appear, and keep the leaves moist.

Ivy requires minimal maintenance. Mow it every other year, just prior to new growth, with the mower at the highest setting. This prevents the growth from becoming so dense that it can harbor undesirable animal life such as snails, slugs, and rats. Watch plants for leaf spot, which begins as ¼-inch, brown or black spots. Generally, this is not serious, but if spots become unsightly, spray the affected area with a fungicide containing copper.

You also should be aware of climate considerations. In hot, dry regions, care includes watering ivy much as you would water a lawn. In colder areas, consider the exposure of the plants: a combination of winter sun and frozen soil results in frost damage. Exposure to a drying winter wind produces the same result. Wiltpruf or a similar antitranspirant can be helpful.

English ivy and Algerian ivy are hardy to −10°F.

Uses: In addition to its versatility and beauty as a ground cover in small- to large-scale plantings, including use as a lawn substitute, carpeting beneath shade trees, and protective covering for slopes, ivy can climb anything and is used in topiary, bonsai, and as a hanging basket and container plant (see the chapter "Using Ground Covers Imaginatively").

This entry was compiled in part from written material provided by American Ivy Society President Henri K. E. Schaepman and Communications Director Rona Schaepman.

Helianthemum
(Sun Rose)

Helianthemum nummularium is a hardy, evergreen, spreading plant that makes an excellent ground cover, particularly if a low-maintenance garden is desired. A vigorous, long-lived native of the Mediterranean region, it has adapted to dry summers. Its height is usually 6 to 8 inches, though some plants reach 1 foot. Each plant ultimately forms a clump about 3 feet in diameter. Branches root as they spread, eventually creating a thick mat. Leaves are narrow, growing to 1 inch in length, and are glossy or dull green, depending on the variety. Bright, 1- to 2-

inch flowers are single or double and come in shades of pink, red, and yellow. The blossoms are delicate and last only a day, but enough flowers on a plant open over a long period that their short life goes unnoticed.

Culture: Sun roses need full sun and neutral-to-alkaline soil. To grow them in high rainfall, acid soil areas, amend the soil with lime before planting. Otherwise these plants are very undemanding, growing better in relatively dry, unfertile soil. They can adapt to wet areas if the drainage is excellent. Shear sun roses in the spring, after the first flowering, to stimulate growth for late summer bloom and to keep the plants dense and compact. Transplanting can be difficult—purchase rooted cuttings if possible and plant 12 to 18 inches apart. Sun roses rarely tolerate root disturbance once they are established, so don't try to cultivate around them or transplant. Where winters are cold and there is no snow cover, insulate with straw or similar material to protect from desiccating winter winds. Propagate with cuttings from new spring growth (late June) or by division. Hardy to −20°F.

Uses: Sun roses do very well in rock gardens, either cascading over and around rocks or tucked into pockets. A close relative of the rock roses (*Cistus*), they also have fire-retardant properties.

Helianthemum nummularium

Hemerocallis 'Hypericon' (left and right)

Hemerocallis
(Daylily)

There aren't many plants as tough and pest-free as the daylilies. They grow in nearly any soil or climate and fit into the landscape in many ways. Insects and diseases leave them alone. Best of all, they offer spectacular and fragrant flowers. If you choose varieties carefully, you can manage to have daylilies in flower from May to October in the mildest climates, perhaps a month or so less in cold regions. Some are repeat bloomers; some bloom in the evening.

Flower colors range from the original yellow, orange, rust, and red to hybrids in pink, vermillion, buff, apricot, white, and two-color varieties. Flower size runs from 3 to 8 inches, and height ranges from the 12-inch dwarfs up to 6 feet. There are both evergreen daylilies for warm climates and deciduous types that grow nearly anywhere.

Daylilies are a collector's plant. To learn more about them, contact the American Hemerocallis Society, Signal Mountain, Tennessee 37377.

Culture: Daylilies can be moved any time of year but the best time is in spring. Plant them on 2-foot centers in a good, well-drained soil. The plants do not need a great deal of water, but apply plenty before and during bloom to insure the best flowering. Apply a balanced type of fertilizer in spring and early summer. Daylilies can be left in place indefinitely without attention, but they perform better if divided every 4 to 6 years. This also increases your supply of plants and provides some to share. Dig the entire clump in early spring or late fall. (Fall is preferable with deciduous varieties since you'll find them more easily than if you wait until they're completely dormant.) Using two spading forks, plunge the tines of both into the center of the clump, then pull the handles to pry the clump into 2, 3, or 4 parts. Replant these divisions with the top of the fleshy roots at soil level. Hardy to −35°F.

Uses: The uses of daylilies are varied. Some, such as *Hemerocallis fulva* 'Europa', are so tough they can reclaim poor or damaged soil, grow by railroad tracks, or hold river banks. Another tough daylily is *H. fulva* 'Kwanso', which is often used along country lanes to naturalize.

Daylilies make excellent cut flowers. Choose a stem with several ready-to-bloom buds. In the house the buds will open, one per day, lasting only a day. Translated from the Greek, hemerocallis means "beautiful for the day."

Daylilies are edible too. Dip the fresh flower buds in egg batter and deep-fry them.

Herniaria
(Rupturewort)

Rupturewort (*Herniaria glabra*) is a trailing herb that forms a dense, glossy green carpet 2 to 4 inches high. In warm climates, it is grown as an evergreen perennial; in cool areas, foliage turns bronzy red in winter; and in cold areas, the plant is treated as an annual. Rupturewort grows slowly; it spreads by rooting stems.

Culture: This plant grows in sun or light shade and in most well-drained soils. It needs regular watering. Propagate by division, spacing divided plants 6 to 8 inches apart. Hardy to −20°F.

Uses: Because it forms a dense, low mat, rupturewort is ideal between stepping-stones, particularly red brick pavers. It takes light traffic.

Heuchera
(Coralbells)

Coralbells (*Heuchera sanguinea*) are evergreen perennials popular throughout the country. They are not a large-scale ground cover but are well suited for brightening small spots. The flowers are bell-shaped, either coral pink or red, and

Herniaria glabra

about ½ inch long. They are borne on 2-foot stalks that appear first in June and last until September. In mild-winter areas, the plants may bloom all year. Evergreen leaves are roundish and are tinged red in winter. The roots are long and fleshy. There are many cultivars available, usually varying in flower color. Hardy to −35°F.

Culture: Coralbells have few problems and usually can be left to take care of themselves for extended periods of time. Soil should be well-drained and moist. Some shade is best, with protection provided from hot afternoon sun. Plant coralbells 1 foot apart in spring in cold areas (protect with a mulch in winter), anytime elsewhere. Don't plant too deep or crowns may rot. To propagate, divide clumps or take a leaf cutting with a small portion of the stem attached. Plants need to be divided when they become woody and produce few flowers. Extend the blooming period by removing faded flowers.

Uses: Coralbells make a distinctive ground cover for small areas. They are good edging plants for perennial borders in which roses, delphiniums, peonies, and similar plants grow. They are favored plants of hummingbirds and are attractive as cut flowers.

Heuchera sanguinea × maxima

Hosta undulata

Hosta
(Plantain Lily, Funkia)

The plantain lilies are a large and valuable group of deciduous perennials valued mainly for their dramatic foliage. They're hardy, long-lived, and one of the best plants to grow in shade. All varieties are deciduous—they die to the ground each winter and are renewed every spring.

The blunt plantain lily (*Hosta decorata*) has oval leaves about 6 inches long. The tips are blunt or abruptly pointed, and 8 to 10 parallel veins are prominent. Two-inch-long, bell-shaped flowers are dark blue-purple, appearing in summer on thin stalks. The cultivar 'Royal Standard' is slightly taller and has long-stemmed flowers.

The narrow-leafed plantain lily (*H. lancifolia*) is one of the lower-growing plantain lilies. Leaves are narrow, shorter (4 inches), and pointed. Flowers, which appear in summer, are a light shade of blue purple.

Fragrant plantain lily (*H. plantaginea*) has 10-inch leaves and large flowers (4 to 5 inches) that are known for their fragrance. They appear in late summer or early fall.

The most impressive leaves belong to *H. sieboldiana*. They are blue green, 10 to 15 inches long, and heavily veined. The flowers are much less significant—they're small (1½ inches long) and set on stalks usually shorter that the leaves. This species makes a dramatic accent by a shaded pool. Several varieties are grown. The leaves of 'Frances Williams' are bordered in a yellow cream color.

Wavy-leafed plantain lily (*H. undulata*) makes taller mounds (to 3 feet) than most types. It also tolerates more sun. It is popular for its 6-inch, variegated, wavy leaves, often used in floral arrangements. Pale lavender, 2-inch flowers appear on 3-foot stalks in summer.

A hybrid plantain lily named 'Honeybells' has the most outstanding flowers of the group. They bloom late on 3-foot stalks and are more open, much like Easter lilies. The lavender-lilac blossoms are also very fragrant.

Culture: Hostas are easy to grow. They prefer a sandy or loamy soil that is high in organic matter and has good drainage. Medium to dense shade is a necessity. To propagate, dig and divide plants when growth first begins in spring. Bait for snails and slugs—they love the leaves. Hostas perform best in cold-winter areas. They are very hardy (to about −30°F). *H. decorata* is somewhat less hardy, tolerating temperatures to −10°F.

Uses: Plantain lilies make excellent border plants and have long been used to edge perennial beds and shrubs. Where shade is heavy, as it can be under trees or facing a northern exposure, these plants are of great practical value. Used singly as accent plants, plantain lilies break up the monotony of too many smaller-leafed plants.

Juniperus
(Junipers)

Few ground covers have as many desirable qualities as the prostrate junipers. They are evergreen, sturdy, and require very little maintenance. They are a difficult-to-resist planting choice, even where other plants might do just as well.

The San Jose juniper (*Juniperus chinensis* 'San Jose') is an excellent, sturdy, semiprostrate juniper with upward-spreading branches to 12 inches high and 6 feet across. The foliage is compact and sage green. This juniper can be used effectively on steep slopes as well as flat areas.

The cultivar *J. c. sargentii* 'Glauca' grows into a low mat 8 to 10 feet across and 10 inches high. Small, scalelike, somewhat feathery foliage is a distinctive blue green. Native to coastal Japan, this plant often is used in coastal areas. *J. c. sargentii* 'Viridis' is the same form with rich green foliage. All these junipers are hardy to −25°F.

The variety *J. communis saxatilis* is a prostrate juniper with upward-spreading branchlets to 1 foot high and 6 feet across. The gray green foliage is composed of prickly clusters of tiny needle-leaves. Hardy to −25°F.

The shore juniper *J. conferta* 'Blue Pacific' is a handsome, low creeper native to coastal Japan. It has compact, blue green, somewhat prickly foliage. One plant grows to 10 feet wide and about 10 inches high. An obvious choice for coastal areas and sandy soils, it also can be grown successfully inland, given enough water. It looks particularly attractive when allowed to cascade over low stone or cement walls. Hardy to −20°F.

The creeping juniper (*J. horizontalis*) is commonly available in many forms. Following are brief descriptions of the more popular cultivars:

'Blue Chip' is a low, mounding juniper with scalelike, silver blue foliage. It grows about 8 inches high and spreads about 2 feet. This variety makes a very effective border. Hardy to −25°F.

'Bar Harbor' is a juniper of striking architectural character. Its flat-branching growth habit is distinctive, and the gray green, not-too-dense, feathery foliage allows some of the main stems to show through. This variety is very effective planted among large, low rocks. In winter, foliage turns to a silvery plum color. Hardy to −25°F.

'Emerson's Creeper' is a moderately dense, low-branching creeper to about 8 inches high and 6 to 8 feet wide. Scalelike foliage is gray green. Hardy to −25°F.

'Emerald Spreader' has a more delicate appearance than most junipers. The foliage is feathery, emerald green, and lightly branched. It grows to about 10 inches high, spreading 4 to 6 feet. Hardy to −25°F.

'Turquoise Spreader' differs from 'Emerald Spreader' in two characteristics: the foliage is denser and has a bluish cast.

'Hughes' is a vigorous, widely spreading juniper with upward-turning branches to 15 inches high. Gray green leaves have a bluish cast and are somewhat needlelike. Hardy to −35°F.

'Douglasii', the Waukegan juniper, is a sturdy ground cover with a semi-erect trailing habit and bluish green, scalelike foliage that has a slight purplish hue in winter. Its mature height is 12 to 16 inches; it spreads 10 feet. It is used like 'Bar Harbor' but is more hardy, to −35°F.

'Plumosa Compacta' is a more compact form of the Andorra juniper (*J. horizontalis* 'Plumosa'). It's similar to 'Douglasii' but has smaller, more feathery, bluish green leaves that turn purple in the winter. Branchlets are more upright than 'Douglasii', reaching 10 to 12 inches, and its spread is less (2 to 4 feet). It is equally hardy, to −35°F.

'Wiltonii', the Wilton carpet juniper, is the lowest- and probably slowest-growing of all ground cover junipers. A spread of 3 feet after 6 years of growth is typical. Also called 'Blue Rug', its trailing, creeping habit and dense, feathery, silver blue foliage forms a 4-inch mat. Use on banks or trailing over walls. Hardy to −25°F.

The dwarf Japanese garden juniper, popularly sold as *J. procumbens* 'Nana', is known botanically as *J. chinensis procumbens* 'Nana'. It's a low-growing, prostrate juniper native to Japan. Foliage is bluish green, dense, and somewhat prickly. The plant's growth habit is creeping; its height builds up to about 6 inches. This is a good rock garden juniper. Another cultivar,

Several varieties of Juniperus horizontalis

Lamium maculatum 'Album'

soil often ends in disappointment. Where clay or other heavy soil is prevalent, it should be amended. Junipers need full sun. Some shade is tolerated, but the plants become woody and lose color. Extra care should be taken in spacing plants—often they are placed too close together. Junipers are slow growers, but a plant that looks harmlessly small in a 1-gallon container ultimately can spread 10 feet in each direction. The tendency to plant more than is necessary is hard to resist. If fast coverage is important, be prepared to remove plants at a later date to avoid crowding.

Despite their sturdy constitution, insects can be troublesome for junipers. A dry, faded look with patchy brown spots on the top of a plant suggests an infestation of spider mites, with large numbers of minute spiders draining the plant's vigor. A growing-season oil spray combined with an insecticide such as malathion controls these pests. A similar treatment is also effective against scale insects, including pine needle scale and juniper scale.

In the West, the juniper twig girdler is harmful to low-growing junipers. The damage is caused by insect larvae that burrow inside the twigs. Two applications of a lindane insecticide are recommended; check the product label.

'Variegata', is the same except for a higher, slightly mounding habit and gray green foliage with patches of light yellow. Both cultivars are hardy to −25°F.

The savin juniper (*J. sabina*) is available in several good ground cover forms:

'Broadmoor' grows compactly to 1 foot. Its leaves are tiny, scalelike, green, and prickly.

'Buffalo' is widely spreading, soft, and feathery. Bright green foliage gives this juniper a striking appearance. It grows 10 to 12 inches high and spreads 4 to 6 feet.

'Arcadia' is more shrublike than most junipers considered to be ground covers. Foliage is rich green and lacy. Upward-rising branches spread to 4 feet and reach a height of 20 inches. This juniper is excellent for spot planting.

'Blue Danube', a native of Austria, has lacy, blue green foliage. Branches grow upward to about 1 foot and spread 4 feet. Use it either as a ground cover or low shrub.

'Scandia' is a rugged, hardy juniper with graceful, spreading branches (to 3 feet) and dense, lacy, yellow green foliage. Its height is about 1 foot. It makes an

excellent ground cover when mass-planted.

'Tamariscifolia' is the well-known tamarix, or simply "tam," juniper. Arching branches carry dense, lacy, blue green foliage suggestive of delicate reef coral. It has a mounding (to 20 inches), symmetrical growth habit and spreads to 4 feet. This juniper is widely used on slopes, set among rocks, and as a mass planting. It is the least hardy of the savin group—to −15°F; others are hardy to −25°F.

J. squamata expansa 'Parsonii' is a handsome, low-growing, densely branched juniper with relatively thick, gray green, scalelike leaves. It grows 6 to 10 inches high and spreads 4 to 6 feet. Hardy to −25°F.

J. virginiana prostrata 'Silver Spreader' is a low-growing form of the red cedar tree. Foliage is silvery green and feathery. Branches are upward-rising to a height of 20 inches and spread to 4 to 6 feet. This juniper makes a good accent plant.

Culture: Growing ground cover junipers successfully can be narrowed down to three elements: good drainage, full sun, and proper spacing. Attempting to grow junipers in heavy, slow-draining

Lamium
(Dead Nettle)

White or yellow splotches along the leaf midrib are the most significant feature of spotted dead nettle (*Lamium maculatum*). It grows to 6 or 8 inches, and the leaves are 1½ inches long. At any time from spring to early summer, purple flowers appear. In fall, the leaves become pink to purple. The plant is fast-growing and roots as it spreads. The cultivar 'Aureum' has leaves splotched with yellow. The species *L. galeobdolon* (also known as *Lamiastrum galeobdolon*) has yellow flower spikes and silvery marked leaves and is commonly known as yellow arch-angel. These plants are hardy but lose their leaves in the coldest winters.

Culture: Lamiums prefer shady spots but tolerate full sun if the soil holds enough water. Once the plants are established, little attention is required. Propagate by division or seeds. Hardy to −20°F.

Uses: The colorful leaves of these plants make them useful for highlighting shaded or quiet corners and for contrasting with the solid green leaves of surrounding plants.

Lavandula angustifolia

Lantana
(Trailing Lantana)

Trailing lantana (*Lantana montevidensis* or sometimes *L. sellowiana*) is a perennial, evergreen shrub in areas where temperatures do not fall much below freezing. Its popularity is due in large part to its general toughness, rapid growth, and recurring display of lavender flowers throughout the year. One-inch clusters of tiny flowers appear along the ends of vinelike stems lined with oval,

Lantana montevidensis

dark green, 1-inch leaves. The stems, 3 to 4 feet long, root as they spread, and the plant grows to a height of 1½ to 2 feet. A number of varieties are available in different colors.

Culture: Trailing lantana seems to need sun to thrive. It grows well in poor soil and is drought-resistant, needing only occasional watering. Old stands get woody and develop dead patches that should be cut in early spring. Whiteflies pester lantana but are easily controlled with Orthene. Hardy to 25°F.

Uses: Trailing lantana is good for large-scale planting, particularly on steep banks where maintenance is a problem. It is perhaps too coarse in texture for covering larger areas around a home. It is useful as an accent plant for borders and edging.

Lavandula
(English Lavender)

English lavender (*Lavandula angustifolia*) has been cultivated for centuries as an ornamental herb and for its aromatic oil. Recently, dwarf varieties have been developed that, in addition to their delightful fragrance, make attractive ground covers. These varieties have characteristics in common: lance-shaped, green gray leaves 1 to 2 inches long; ½-inch-wide, blue to purple flowers in spikes on long stems 8 inches to 2 feet tall; and a

moderate growth rate. They grow in clumps 1 to 2 feet wide and bloom about 2 months in midsummer.

Following is a listing of several lavender cultivars and their distinctive characteristics:

'Carroll Gardens': pale purple flowers.

'Compacta': compact habit to 8 inches high.

'Dutch': deep blue flowers.

'Fragrance': heavily scented.

'Hidcote': deep purple flowers, 12 inches high.

'Munstead': lilac blue flowers, early blooming.

'Twickel Purple': dark purple flowers in fanlike clusters.

Culture: English lavender needs full sun and average, but well-drained soil to thrive. It can be propagated by seeds or division, or by rooting 2- to 5-inch cuttings or new shoots. Set rooted plants 2 feet apart. Established plants can be sheared in early spring to induce dense growth, but after 3 to 4 years plants become leggy and the best thing to do is to take them out and replant. Hardy to −15°F.

Uses: As a ground cover, English lavender is an excellent choice. It is a natural for borders and in rock and herb gardens. Its fragrance is also an asset.

Beyond these uses, all varieties provide delightful cut flowers. Lavender sachets also can be made. Collect and dry the flower heads just as the flowers start to open. Though not as potent, leaves and stems contain the scent and can be used also. The fragrance is very subtle, so use at least one-third cup for each sachet. If the scent becomes too faint, simply crush the sachet in your hand to release the fragrance again. Use lavender to scent sheets, pillows, towels, even stationery.

Liriope
(Lilyturf)

Liriope is characterized by clumps of coarse, mostly dark green, grasslike leaves up to 24 inches long and ¼ to ¾ inch wide. Like ophiopogon, with which it is sometimes confused, it is a member of the lily family. One difference between the two is that liriope is hardier.

Big blue lilyturf (*Liriope muscari*) gets its name from its 4- to 8-inch-long, spikelike clusters of flowers that are, in fact, more violet than blue. The flowers appear in good number among the leaves from about July into September and are followed by a few blue black berries. This is the tallest of the lilyturfs, growing rather slowly to a height of 2 feet. It is sometimes listed as *Ophiopogon jaburan*.

Creeping lilyturf (*L. spicata*) is smaller in all aspects, forms a dense cover

Lobularia maritima

that spreads by underground stems, has pale lavender flowers, and grows at a moderate rate up to 1 foot high.

Culture: These plants have no special soil or light requirements but probably are grown more often in partial shade, if only for reasons of landscape design. They need only light summer watering. Both species are easily propagated by division. In extremely cold weather the leaves of both plants turn

yellow and should be clipped off before new growth starts in spring. *L. spicata* is the hardiest, tolerating temperatures to −20°F. *L. muscari* is damaged by temperatures below 0°F.

Uses: These plants are excellent as borders along paths, under trees, and in rock gardens, or as fill-in ground cover in small areas.

Lobularia
(Sweet Alyssum)

Sweet alyssum (*Lobularia maritima*) is a common late fall (in mild climates) or early spring bedding plant not usually considered a ground cover. It is commonly used with a new ground cover planting to cover and protect the bare soil while the planting is becoming established. It's very low-growing (rarely more than 1 foot) and has narrow, gray green leaves. Quarter-size flowers appear in clusters all season long. Colors vary between dark purple and white. Some of the best cultivars are 'Carpet of Snow', white flowers and 4 inches tall; 'Tiny Tim', white flowers and 2 or 3 inches tall; and 'Oriental Night', dark purple flowers and 4 inches tall.

Culture: In mild areas, treat sweet alyssum as a short-lived perennial and spread seeds or set out small plants as needed. In cold climates, plant in early spring for summer bloom. Full sun (some shade is all right), average soil, and regular watering are all that is necessary for them to thrive.

Uses: Sweet alyssum has many garden uses: as a low border, between steps, and in containers. As mentioned, it is a good plant to use among slower-growing ground cover plants that haven't yet formed a tight, weed-free mat.

Liriope muscari

Lonicera japonica 'Halliana'

Lotus berthelotii

Lonicera
(Honeysuckle)

Of the many species of honeysuckle, most are vines, a few are shrubs, and one, Hall's Japanese honeysuckle (*Lonicera japonica* 'Halliana'), though essentially a vine, is used as a ground cover. It is evergreen in mild climates and semi-evergreen or deciduous in colder climates. It has the typical twining, climbing (if allowed) honeysuckle growth habit; soft, downy, green leaves; and fragrant, trumpet-shaped, white flowers that appear in summer and turn a colorful yellow with age. It is exceptionally fast-growing, spreading rapidly by stems that root as they cover the ground. In a flat area it can be expected to mound up to 6 feet. Because of its invasive nature, it has become a pest in some parts of the country. Other cultivars are 'Aureo-reticulata', a less vigorous grower, which is called the yellownet honeysuckle because of its yellow-veined leaves; and 'Purpurea', which has purple-tinged leaves and flowers that are purple outside and white inside.

Culture: These honeysuckles grow in most soils in sun or light shade and are drought-resistant. They are easily propagated by division or cuttings. Honeysuckle becomes very woody and scraggly if not cut back. Hardy to $-20°F$.

Uses: These plants are useful for any informal, medium-to-large area where they cannot strangle shrubs or climb trees.

Lotus
(Parrot's-beak)

Parrot's-beak (*Lotus berthelotii*) is a low-growing plant 3 to 4 inches high with trailing, flat branches covered with clusters of soft, needlelike leaves ¾ inch long. The vinelike branches are a powder gray brown and the leaves a silvery green, creating a handsome color effect. Brilliant, deep scarlet flowers with petals shaped somewhat like a parrot's beak appear in profusion from late spring into summer. Mow the plant to create a smooth, green carpet. A related plant is bird's-foot trefoil (*L. corniculatus*), which is much hardier (to $-25°F$) and grows easily on dry banks.

Culture: Give this plant full sun, a well-drained soil, and moderate to light watering. Propagate by division or cuttings. Hardy to $30°F$.

Uses: Parrot's-beak is delightful draping over walls or hanging from a basket. On a larger scale, it makes an excellent bank cover.

Lysimachia
(Moneywort, Creeping Jennie)

Moneywort (*Lysimachia nummularia*) belongs with those rapidly spreading creepers that are weeds where you don't

Lysimachia nummularia

Mazus reptans

want them (in a lawn) and ground covers where you do. This one has small, bright green, rounded leaves on delicate rooting stems. The leaves, set opposite each other, grow in sufficient number to form a wavy carpet a few inches high. Bright yellow flowers about ¾ inch in diameter appear through the summer.

Culture: Moneywort grows almost anyplace, in sun or shade, provided the soil is moist to wet. Propagate by division, starting new plants at any time. Hardy to −40°F.

Uses: Grow moneywort in moist, shady places where other plants, such as grass, won't grow. A natural place would be around small pools with rock sites for the foliage to creep over. Moneywort tolerates light traffic.

Mahonia
(Creeping Mahonia)

Creeping mahonia (*Mahonia repens*) retains many of the characteristics of the larger mahonia species, specifically Oregon grape (*M. aquifolium*), that make them especially interesting landscape subjects. It has striking bluish green, spiny, hollylike leaves and 1- to 3-inch clusters of bright yellow flowers in spring. After the flowers fall, dark purple, grape-like berries form. The plant grows 1 to 2 feet high and spreads rapidly by underground stems.

Culture: Creeping mahonia can be planted in full sun, but it grows equally well, and looks better, in filtered shade. It deserves a good, somewhat moist soil. It can be propagated by division or from root cuttings (space the rooted plants about 10 inches apart in spring). Hardy to −10°F.

Uses: This is a plant for medium and small areas, including borders and patio settings with rocks and lattice.

Mahonia repens

Mazus
(Mazus)

Mazus reptans is a perennial herb that forms a thick, low mat only 1 or 2 inches high. It spreads rapidly, rooting along its stems, and sends up small, purplish blue flowers spotted yellow and white from late spring into summer. It is evergreen in warm-winter areas; elsewhere it freezes to the ground in winter but recovers quickly in the spring.

Culture: This alpine plant grows best in a good, moist soil in sun or shade. Propagate by division. Hardy to −40°F.

Uses: Ths plant is particularly attractive for small-scale planting in beds, around walks, and as edging. It takes light traffic.

Mentha
(Corsican Mint)

Corsican mint (*Mentha requienii*) is the lowest-growing of the many species and dozens of cultivars of mint. It spreads rapidly by underground stems, forming a soft, green carpet 1 to 3 inches high. Tiny, oval leaves, about ⅛ inch across, grow opposite one another on slender stems and give off a strong minty fragrance when bruised. Tiny, lavender flowers appear in midsummer.

Culture: This plant grows equally well in sun or light shade. In a well-drained, fairly rich soil kept on the moist side, it is a vigorous grower. It is easily propagated by division; set new plants 6 inches apart. Corsican mint self-sows. If exposed to freezing temperatures for any period of time, it will seem to disappear but usually returns in the spring. Hardy to 0°F.

Uses: Corsican mint makes a delightful ground cover for small patches anywhere in the garden, especially between steppingstones. When you step on it, the delightfully fresh peppermint scent is released. In Corsica, where this plant is native, the fragrance fills the air.

Mentha requienii

Myoporum
(Prostrate Myoporum)

Prostrate myoporum (*Myoporum parvifolium*) is a fresh-looking, evergreen shrub, highly rated for coastal California. It grows 3 to 6 inches high and spreads 5 feet or more by means of long, trailing stems. Small, white flowers appear in summer, but it is the foliage and growth form that make the plant such an attractive ground cover. The bright green leaves, ½ to 1 inch long and closely set along the branches, literally sparkle in the sun. The branches themselves trail gracefully along the ground, rooting where the nodes contact moist soil. This plant is for warm-weather climates. Its growth is quite rapid—up to 3 feet in the first year from transplants.

Culture: Although *M. parvifolium* is grown successfully in many areas of southern and central California, it does best at the seashore, benefiting from the relatively cool temperatures and high humidity during the summer months. The plant has good drought tolerance and is undamaged by salt spray from the ocean. The main problem in hot, inland areas is its poor heat tolerance. Stands tend to become yellow and patchy during the hottest part of the year, even if they're watered enough. Well-drained soil is a must. Plants can be started from tip cuttings or by dividing rooted branches. Set 2 to 3 feet apart to give rapid, dense cover. In confined areas, plantings need to be edged 2 or 3 times a year; otherwise maintenance is low. *M. parvifolium* does not tolerate cold.

Uses: Few plants are better or more attractive than *M. parvifolium* for erosion control and fire-hazard reduction on hillside areas along the coast where some summer irrigation can be provided. The plant is tough but does not take traffic. It is well suited for large-scale landscaping and is neat enough to be used in small, semiformal plantings adjacent to lawns or as cover between flowering trees, on banks, and around patios.

Nandina
(Heavenly Bamboo)

Heavenly bamboo (*Nandina domestica*) is a well-known landscape shrub that gardeners have favored for many years. A new cultivar, 'Harbor Dwarf', introduced by Georgia's Calloway Gardens, is very

Myoporum parvifolium (left and right)

Nepeta mussinii

slow until the plant is well established. 'Nana' is a dwarf cultivar of *O. japonicus*, growing about half as high.

O. jaburan is similar in size and growth habit to *Liriope muscari*, each plant often being taken for the other. The chief observable differences are that *O. jaburan* has green instead of brownish stems, and white, more drooping, less tightly clustered flowers. *O. jaburan* 'Variegatus' is a low-growing cultivar with white, striated leaves.

Culture: These plants are adaptable to most well-drained soils. In coastal areas they grow in full sun; elsewhere they look and grow best in partial shade. In all areas, regular summer watering is required. Mondo grass needs more frequent watering if exposed to full sun in a mass planting. New plants can be started by dividing clumps; set the plants 6 inches apart (12 inches apart for *O. jaburan*). Hardy to about 0°F.

Uses: Mondo grass looks good as a sizable planting under the shade of a large tree. In a shaded patio setting, a few dozen plants, placed about 8 inches apart with baby's-tears (*Soleirolia soleirolii*) in between, produce a lovely, cool effect. These plants also make a handsome border along paths and are useful in defining and separating a lawn and flower bed. *O. jaburan* is most effective where its attractive flowers (good for cutting) and violet blue fruits can be seen up close, as in entryways, near fences or buildings, and under trees.

low (12 to 18 inches high), dense, and spreading. It is semideciduous as hardiness limits are reached (0°F) and evergreen in mild climates. The plant is orange to bronzy red in fall and a soft, green-tinted pink in spring.

Culture: Nandinas tolerate some shade, but foliage colors more dramatically when the plants are grown in full sun. Rich, well-drained soil is best, with plenty of water through the summer.

Uses: The lacy, bamboolike foliage and spreading habit combine to make 'Harbor Dwarf' a very unusual, medium-height ground cover. Use it near the house or where it can be appreciated up close. It's also used as a low hedge and a container plant.

Nepeta
(Persian Catmint)

Persian catmint (*Nepeta mussinii*) has year-round foliage of small, sturdy, gray green leaves that make this herb an attractive ground cover, enhanced in early summer by a lush production of lavender flower spikes on stems 1 to 2 feet high.

Culture: Persian catmint requires a light, well-drained soil, full sun, and periodic watering in the summer. If dead flower spikes are removed after spring blooms, a second bloom usually occurs in the fall. Hardy to −20°F.

Uses: This plant is most attractive in large patches in a rock garden, as a border, or behind a low-growing cover such as rupturewort (*Herniaria glabra*). Cats like to roll in Persian catmint as much as they do in the standard catnip, *N. cataria*.

Ophiopogon
(Mondo Grass)

Mondo grass (*Ophiopogon japonicus*) is the most grasslike of the lilyturfs. It is identified by dense clumps of long, ⅛-inch-wide leaves that arch over into mounds 8 to 10 inches high. The leaves are dark green and coarse in texture. Small, pale purple flowers, mostly hidden among the leaves, appear in July and August, followed by pea-size blue fruit. Mondo grass spreads by means of fleshy, subsurface stems. The growth rate is quite

Ophiopogon japonicus

Pachysandra
(Japanese Spurge)

Japanese spurge (*Pachysandra terminalis*) is an evergreen perennial widely used throughout the world as a ground cover in shady locations. It remains evergreen in the most severe winters. Veined, dark green, oval leaves, 1½ to 4 inches long and lightly toothed near the ends, grow in clusters at the top of upright stems 6 to 8 inches high. The plant spreads rapidly by underground runners to form a dense cover of essentially uniform height. The cultivar 'Green Carpet' is darker green with more flowers.

Culture: Japanese spurge grows only in filtered to full shade and performs best in good, somewhat moist, acidic soil. New plants can be started by division or rooted cuttings that are spaced 6 to 12 inches apart in spring. Hardy to −30°F.

Uses: This is the perfect ground cover to use as a large-scale planting under trees or, on a small scale, in the shade of evergreen shrubs.

Parthenocissus
(Virginia Creeper, Woodbine)

Parthenocissus quinquefolia is a rambling, deciduous vine native to eastern North America. It is common to woodlands and is especially visible in the fall, when it turns bright red. Boston ivy (*P. tricuspidata*) is a close relative. The leaves are divided into leaflets that are each attached at the same point and are 2 to 6 inches long, depending on the variety. The leaflets are heavily veined and have toothed edges. The cultivar *P. q.* 'Englemannii' has smaller leaflets. Inconspicuous flowers are followed by attractive blue fruits that are loved by birds.

Pachysandra terminalis (left and right)

Culture: Virginia creeper is fast and easy to grow. Spaced widely, it covers a large area cheaply and remarkably fast, though not very densely. Spaced closely (3 to 5 feet apart) in rich, moist soil, the plants can make a solid cover in one season. Virginia creeper takes some shade. It propagates easily by layers that form naturally or with your help and also can be grown from spring-sown seed. Hardy to −35°F.

Uses: Virginia creeper readily climbs trellises and drapes over walls, attaching itself to objects by means of adhesive discs. Be careful—don't plant where it can climb (and maybe smother) shrubs or trees. It is best used to cover large, barren, rocky areas where little else grows and makes an excellent slope cover. It is also well suited to naturalistic areas, where its growth doesn't need to be controlled.

Paxistima
(Canby, Pachistima)

Canby (*Paxistima canbyi*) is a 1-foot-high, low-maintenance ground cover. It has been known but little used for many years and is native to the mountains of Virginia and the Carolinas. Similar to boxwood, it has narrow, ¼-inch wide and ¼- to 1-inch-long, evergreen leaves that color slightly in cold-winter areas. The plant becomes dense and is long-lived.

Oregon boxwood (*P. myrsinites*) is native to the West Coast. Its leaves are slightly larger and it can become twice as tall as *P. canbyi*, but it is easily kept low with pruning. Cool, moist areas in full sun are ideal, making the plant well suited to coastal locations; but it can be grown inland with some shade and lots of water.

Culture: Canby grows well in either

Paxistima canbyi

full sun or partial shade, although it usually becomes denser in full sun. It's native to rocky soil, but any well-drained, slightly acidic garden soil is satisfactory. Branches root as they spread. Propagate by division or cuttings. Hardy to −10°F.

Uses: Canby grows well under trees and as a low hedge. It is also a good choice for naturalistic and rock gardens.

Pernettya
(Pernettya)

Pernettya mucronata is a handsome, dwarf evergreen shrub much admired for its white to dark purple, ½-inch-wide berries that appear in great number from autumn through winter. The berries are preceded by a fine display of tiny, white, bell-shaped flowers. Berries and flowers are set off by small, shiny, dark green leaves that turn bronze in winter. The shrub spreads by underground runners, forming wide clumps up to 1½ feet.

Culture: Except in hot areas, pernettya is best grown in full sun; in shade it tends to become rank and invasive. It needs an acid soil and generally cool, moist conditions. It is a good idea to group several of the color varieties together to insure cross-pollination and an ample production of fruit. Propagate by division or cuttings. Hardy to −5°F.

Uses: This plant is effective as a border near an entryway or along a path; it is also attractive as a hedge adjoining a garden pool.

Pernettya mucronata

Phalaris arundinacea 'Picta'

Phalaris
(Ribbon Grass)

Ribbon grass (*Phalaris arundinacea* 'Picta') has long been used decoratively. It is hardy everywhere and is tolerant of poor growing conditions. Its height is typically 3 feet, and its leaves are 6 to 12 inches long with white stripes. The top growth browns in fall but remains erect. Unfortunately, ribbon grass spreads by underground runners and is very invasive.

Culture: Easy to grow, ribbon grass is most vigorous in rich, well-drained soil, though leaf variegation may disappear in these conditions. In dry, heavy, or wet soil, growth slows and the plant is more manageable. In a garden, plant ribbon grass in containers such as a section of concrete or clay drain pipe 2½ feet long (width depends on the size of clump desired), which blocks the runners and prevents the plant from taking over the yard. Once established, it is difficult to eradicate unless contained. Hardy to −40°F.

Uses: Ribbon grass is very handsome in a perennial border or as a backdrop for other plants. The foliage is striking from spring to midsummer.

Phlox
(Moss phlox)

Moss phlox (*Phlox subulata*), one of the standard rock garden plants, is a mat-

forming perennial that produces a 4- to 6-inch-high carpet of brilliant color lasting about one month from late spring into midsummer. The ½-inch flowers, ranging in color from white to various shades of pink and red, cover the needlelike foliage completely. Individual plants grow in clumps, spreading rapidly by means of trailing stems. Different-colored cultivars are generally available, including 'White Delight', 'Red Wings', and 'Emerald Blue'.

Culture: Moss phlox is hardy, sturdy, and grows in most soils with good drainage but needs full sun. Because seeds are not reliable in reproducing to type, propagation is best by division. In spring, set out new plants 12 to 18 inches apart. To stimulate growth and keep plants compact, mow them about halfway to the ground after flowering. Hardy to −40°F.

Uses: Besides its familiar use in rock gardens, moss phlox makes an attractive, small-scale border or accent plant. It is also very dramatic and attractive in large-scale plantings.

Phyla
(Lippia)

Phyla nodiflora (also known as *Lippia canescens*) is a perennial, evergreen herb. With some exceptions, it makes an

excellent lawn substitute in warm climates. It forms a dense mat 1 to 2 inches high in the sun and up to 6 inches in the shade. Its green foliage spreads rapidly by surface runners. Tiny, lavender flowers spotted with yellow appear from spring through summer. They attract bees, a liability when using the plant as a lawn substitute.

Culture: Lippia grows well in most soils in sun or partial shade, but better in sun. It withstands extreme heat and sun and is very drought-resistant. Propagate by division, planting small pieces of sod 4 inches apart for fast cover. Hardy to 20°F.

Uses: If the plant's flowers are mowed off, a tough, flat, green mat is left that is very suitable for use as a lawn substitute in an informal setting. Lippia is also effective around small garden pools, where it can creep among rocks and up little slopes.

Pittosporum
(Mock Orange)

Mock orange (*Pittosporum tobira*) is an evergreen shrub or small tree 6 to 15 feet or more high. The cultivar 'Wheeler's Dwarf' grows to about 2 feet and is useful as a ground cover for certain applications. Typically, mock orange has thick, leathery leaves, roughly oval in shape and ¾ to 1½

Phlox subulata (mixed colors)

Phyla nodiflora

characterized by wiry, trailing, reddish stems loosely covered by inch-long, elliptical, dark green to pinkish leaves and small, pink flower heads that bloom most of the year. When planted in a fairly large area, the overall effect is a dull wine-red, tangled ground cover mounding 5 to 8 inches high.

P. vacciniifolium is a taller (to 9 inches), vigorous, less weedy-looking plant than *P. capitatum*, mainly because of its rosy, upright, 3- to 4-inch-long flower spikes.

Japanese knotweed (*P. cuspidatum compactum*) is the hardiest of this group, easily surviving harsh winters in exposed locations. It grows 15 to 18 inches tall and blooms with pink flowers in late summer. Because it is fast-growing and tolerant of poor-soil, it can be terribly invasive. Use it only where it has plenty of room to spread or where its toughness is needed.

Culture: These plants grow best in full sun in any soil that has good drainage. Occasional watering in dry-summer areas is their only maintenance requirement. *P. capitatum* is tender to frost but comes back if the freeze is not too severe. *P. vacciniifolium* is hardy to 5°F and *P. cuspidatum compactum* to −20°F. All three plants are easily propagated by division or cuttings.

Uses: Basically, these plants are suitable for any informal setting as long as they are contained. *P. capitatum* has been used effectively in southern California as a parking strip planting. *P. vacciniifolium* makes a good cover on moderate slopes and can be quite striking in a rock garden.

inches long. They are dark green and densely set along the branches, most heavily at the tips. Orange-scented, white flowers that become cream-colored with age appear in dense clusters at the branch tips in spring. 'Wheeler's Dwarf' has a mounding growth habit and a moderate growth rate. A variegated cultivar is available that grows somewhat higher and is distinguished by light green leaves etched in creamy white at the tips.

Culture: These are sturdy plants that grow well in most soils in full sun or partial shade. They need regular watering throughout the year. Pruning should be kept to a minimum. Propagate by seeds or cuttings. Hardy to 20°F.

Uses: These are popular landscape plants in mild-climate areas, where they are effective as a foreground for taller plants. They also make excellent borders, particularly along steppingstone paths.

Polygonum
(Knotweed, Pink Clover Blossom)

The few species of *Polygonum* that can be said to qualify as ornamental ground covers are mostly mat-forming, creeping perennials that spread rapidly and invasively to the point of being pests. Nonetheless, they can be useful and do have attractive foliage and a long blooming period.

One of the most widely used species is pink clover blossom (*P. capitatum*),

Pittosporum tobira 'Wheeler's Dwarf'

Polygonum capitatum

Polystichum
(Shield Fern)

Polystichum species are a large group of ferns, including many natives of North American forests. They are hardy and usually evergreen with sword-shaped fronds. These plants are similar to dryopteris, but the rough, saw-toothed edges of polystichum fronds are a typical, distinguishing characteristic.

The Christmas fern (*P. acrostichoides*) is native from Nova Scotia to Florida. The common name derives from the commercial availability of its fronds for Christmas decorations. It is also used as a house plant.

The western sword fern (*P. munitum*) is native to an area extending from Alaska south to California and east to Montana. Its fronds are leathery, 2 to 3½ feet long, and sometimes 10 inches wide at the base.

Culture: Moisture, full shade, and a humus-rich soil are the most important needs of shield ferns. Propagate by dividing the underground runners in spring.

Uses: Shady woodlands and rock gardens are the most common places to use these plants.

Potentilla
(Cinquefoil)

The cinquefoils are perennial, mostly evergreen, herbaceous plants that make highly serviceable, ornamental ground covers. They have in common 5 wedge-shaped, bright green, coarsely toothed leaflets; small, roselike flowers; and a rapid growth rate, spreading by surface runners.

Spring cinquefoil (*Potentilla verna*) is the lowest-growing, forming a dense, matlike cover 3 to 6 inches high. Bright yellow, 4-petaled flowers, about ⅜ inch across, appear singly but in great number from spring well into summer.

P. nepalensis 'Willmottiae' grows to 10 inches high, has correspondingly larger leaflets, and flowers that are a striking deep red.

Alpine cinquefoil (*P. cinerea*), popular in the Pacific Northwest, has pale yellow flowers and grows in tufts up to 4 inches high.

Culture: These plants grow in full sun in all but desert areas and also do well in shade. They need a well-drained soil and regular watering. Propagate by division. *P. cinerea* and *P. n.* 'Willmottiae' are the hardiest (to −40°F). *P. verna* is somewhat less hardy (to −10°F).

Uses: Cinquefoils are excellent for medium-scale planting on slopes, under high-branched trees, or among groups of rocks, where the yellow-flowering species give a cheerful feeling and the red-flowering species more drama.

Pyracantha
(Fire Thorn)

The genera *Pyracantha* and *Cotoneaster* are composed of botanically similar evergreen shrubs that are sometimes difficult to distinguish at first glance. The easiest identifiable difference is that most pyracanthas have thorns, whereas most cotoneasters do not. Also, ground cover forms of cotoneaster generally have a more branching, flatter growth habit than similar forms of pyracantha. Beyond this, pyracanthas such as *P. koidzumii* 'Santa Cruz Prostrata' and the hybrid *P.* × 'Ruby Mound' have denser foliage.

P. koidzumii 'Santa Cruz Prostrata' has glossy, dark green, oval leaves 1½ to 2½ inches long and serrated at the tips. Masses of short-lived, tiny, white flowers appear in the spring. In the fall, clusters of bright red, berrylike fruits, attractively framed against the leaves, appear along the branch ends. The fruits remain on the branches for several months. The plant has a prostrate, rapidly spreading growth habit and mounds to 2 to 4 feet in height. 'Ruby Mound' is notable for its long, graceful, intertwining branches. In 5 years a single plant mounds to 2½ feet and spreads to 10 feet.

Culture: These plants grow in most soils, doing best in sunny locations. Al-

Polystichum munitum

Rosa rugosa

Rosa 'Max Graf'

though regular watering is needed, fruit production is stimulated by keeping the soil on the dry side. Except for occasional pruning of upward-growing branches, little maintenance is required. Pyracanthas are subject to attacks of fireblight, a bacterial disease that causes the foliage and stems to turn black, as if burned (see *Cotoneaster* for control methods). They can be propagated by seeds or, more quickly, from cuttings rooted in a light potting mix; in spring, set out rooted plants about 18 inches apart. Hardy to 10°F.

Uses: These decorative plants are excellent as borders, rough hedges, or trailing down rocky slopes. The ripe fruits are edible and can be used to make a bland jelly.

Rosa
(Rose)

There are many roses that can be used as ground covers. Low-growing polyanthas and floribundas can be mass-planted and easily kept to a 3-foot height by occasionally pruning the upright stems. Almost any strong-growing, climbing rose can be pegged down and used as a ground cover also. Tie the long canes at the tips to short stakes. Flower-bearing growth is then forced along the entire length of the cane.

'Max Graf' rose is thought to be a hybrid of *Rosa wichuraiana* and *R. rugosa*. At one time, it was a very popular ground cover. It grows 3 to 4 feet high and is trailing but somewhat bushier than *R. wichuraiana*. Pink, 3-inch flowers with golden centers are produced through the summer. Hardy to −10°F.

R. rugosa is called sea tomato in Japan. A tough rose, it's one of the best seashore plants, withstanding considerable salt spray without damage. Leaves are glossy and leathery, turning orange in fall. Flowers may be single or double and up to 3½ inches in diameter, with many colors available. The tomato-shaped fruits (rose hips) are brick red, about 1 inch wide, and good for making preserves. The spread-

ing, underground roots make it an excellent soil binder for slopes or sandy soil. Hardy to −40°F.

The memorial rose (*R. wichuraiana*) normally grows to only 1 foot high. It's an extremely vigorous, trailing plant that can spread 10 feet in a single season. Growth this fast can cause trouble, so use only in large areas where the plant has plenty of room to ramble. White, 2-inch flowers are produced in summer. Hardy to −20°F.

Culture: These roses grow best in prepared soil and full sun but tolerate poor soil. Propagate by cuttings or by digging the natural layers formed as the trailing stems root. Plant 4 to 5 feet apart for a rapid cover.

Uses: These roses are unsurpassed for rapidly covering large, poor soil areas. Weeds can grow through a ground cover of roses; growth is not dense enough to shade them out.

Pyracantha koidzumii

Rosmarinus
(Dwarf Rosemary)

This woody evergreen is well known in its taller form for its various herbal uses. The creeping *Rosmarinus officinalis* 'Prostratus' grows slowly along the ground, spreading 4 to 8 feet. Its normal height is about 8 inches, but a mass planting can be expected to mound up to 2 feet, particularly as plants mature. 'Prostratus' has the typically aromatic, narrow, deep green leaves and tiny clusters of light blue, 1/2-inch flowers that appear the greater part of the year, most heavily in winter and spring. A cultivar of *R. officinalis* widely used in southern California is 'Lockwood de Forest', developed by a landscape architect after whom it is named. It is similar to 'Prostratus' but has some erect branches that grow to 2 feet and foliage that is somewhat lighter in color.

Culture: Dwarf rosemary grows well in almost any soil as long as it has good drainage; it does not tolerate soggy soil. The plant is drought-tolerant but grows best with some additional water in very dry areas. Little or no fertilizer is needed. Propagate by seeds or by cuttings, setting new plants 2 feet apart. Plants become woody as they get older; control and rejuvenate by cutting out dead wood. Hardy to 10°F.

Uses: Dwarf rosemary is excellent as a border or hedge, cascading over a low wall, or grown on a slope to prevent erosion. As an herb, use rosemary on steak, in spaghetti sauce, and in omelettes (crush and heat with butter).

Sagina
(Irish Moss, Scotch Moss)

Irish moss (*Sagina subulata*) and Scotch moss (*S. subulata* 'Aurea') are evergreen, perennial herbs that are alike except for color. (Both are sometimes called pearlwort.) Irish moss is deep green; Scotch moss is yellow green. They grow in dense, rounded tufts of tiny, awl-shaped leaves. If permitted, the tufts grow together by means of creeping stems, rapidly forming a soft, mossy carpet 3 to 4 inches high. Both produce tiny, white flowers in the summer.

Culture: These plants grow equally well in full sun or light shade. To thrive, they need a rich, well-drained soil and enough water to keep them moist but not soggy. Propagate by division. Hardy to −20°F.

Uses: The growth habit and interesting texture of Irish and Scotch moss make them ideal for use between steppingstones and other places where they can fill in against rocks.

Santolina
(Lavender Cotton)

Lavender cotton (*Santolina chamaecyparissus*) is an evergreen shrub grown chiefly for its distinctive light gray, aromatic foliage. Close inspection reveals finely cut, woolly, green-tinged leaves densely covering the top 6 to 8 inches of woody stems that can rise as high as 2½ feet. For a month or so in the summer, the foliage is partially covered by a profusion of small, round, bright yellow flower heads. Lavender cotton is sturdy and spreads rapidly by creeping stems. A dwarf form, 'Nana', is available in some nurseries. *S. virens* is similar to *S. chamaecyparissus* but has deep green, more delicate foliage and pale yellow flowers. It grows about half as high and is clumpier in form.

Culture: Santolina grows in any well-drained (including sandy or gravelly) soil in full sun. It is exceptionally drought-resistant and requires only occasional watering in the summer. It dies to the ground in very cold areas but usually recovers. To keep foliage compact and to prevent woody stems from showing, the plant should be pruned once a year to 1 foot or less in height. Propagate from cuttings taken in spring or fall. Hardy to 5°F but might be slightly damaged.

Uses: Left untouched, Santolina can serve as an informal planting against a wood fence. Clipped, it can serve as a semiformal, low hedge or as an accent plant in a patio or other small area, in

Sagina subulata 'Aurea'

Santolina chamaecyparissus

which case it rarely flowers. In Europe, sachets made from the dried foliage (very powdery—use tightly woven material) have long been used as a moth repellent.

Sarcococca
(Small Himalayan Sarcococca)

Sarcococca hookeriana humilis is an attractive, broad-leafed, evergreen shrub noteworthy for its adaptability to dense shade. It stays low, rarely exceeding 2 feet, and spreads several feet by underground runners. Its most attractive feature is glossy, dark green foliage. The leaves are 1 to 2 inches long and about ½ inch wide. Fragrant, white flowers in spring are followed by black berries. Hardy to −20°F.

Culture: The most important cultural factors are acidic soil generously amended with organic matter, and shade. Direct sunlight or reflected heat are damaging, as is too much wind. Water frequently until the plant becomes established, then water normally. Pinch stem tips to promote horizontal spreading and dense growth. Propagate by cuttings, seeds, or division of the creeping roots. Check for scale insects.

Uses: This plant is excellent as a mass planting in heavily shaded areas

where little else grows or as a low border in front of such tall-growing shrubs as rhododendrons and camellias.

Sedum
(Stonecrop)

There are more than 300 species and at least twice as many varieties of sedum. There are tiny sedums that form mats only 1 or 2 inches high and others that reach 2 feet. A few flower abundantly; others are shy bloomers. The beauty of the plants is in the shape and color of their leaves.

Sedum acre, known as mossy or gold-moss stonecrop, has tiny leaves less than ¼ inch long. It is vigorous and grows to a height of only 2 inches. It is perfectly happy growing between steppingstones and in rock crevices and stays green

through the coldest of winters. Hardy to −35°F.

S. album is a fast-growing, creeping evergreen that forms a green mat 3 to 6 inches high. In the summer it sends up 8-inch stems covered at the top by delicate, branching clusters of tiny, star-shaped, white flowers that attract bees. There are a number of varieties, some with purple foliage and yellow green or pinkish flowers. Hardy to −20°F.

S. anglicum is a popular, hardy, evergreen creeper that forms a dense, mosslike, dark green mat about 3 inches high. In the summer it sends up 3- to 5-inch stems covered by pinkish white flowers. Hardy to −20°F.

S. brevifolium, an evergreen creeper, forms a bright green mat 2 inches high. It has wiry, somewhat woody stems and, in summer, white flowers streaked with pink. It makes a good rock garden plant. Hardy to −20°F.

S. confusum is a relatively tender sedum. It is an evergreen, somewhat shrubby, branching plant to about 1 foot high. The leaves are light green; the summer flowers are yellow. It is a plant that fills in quickly and makes a good ground cover for level areas or slopes. Hardy to 10°F.

S. dasyphyllum is a handsome evergreen (annual in very cold climates) that forms a low-tufted (1 to 2 inches), bluish green mat lightly covered by white flowers in summer and fall. It needs full sun. Hardy to 0°F.

S. × rubrotinctum, commonly known as pork and beans or whisky nose, is

Sarcococca hookeriana humilis

Sedum × rubrotinctum

Sempervivum × 'Clara Noyes'

Sempervivum hybrids

deservedly popular. Stems are 3 to 6 inches long, the top half covered with clusters of beanlike, green leaves that become bronzy red with exposure to full sun. The plant is excellent in every way sedums can be used. It seeds itself so easily that it can crowd out smaller species. It produces yellow flowers in the spring, but it's the evergreen foliage that recommends it. Hardy to 10°F.

S. *morganianum* is the popular donkey's- or burro's-tail, so named because of a growth habit that produces long (6 inches to 3 feet), trailing stems densely covered with short, fleshy, gray green leaves. It is really not suitable as a standard ground cover, but in mild areas (not reliably hardy below freezing) it can be very effective on a slope, draped over a wall, or as a house plant. In contrast to most sedums, it requires good soil, some shade, and regular watering in the summer. Hardy to 30°F.

S. *oaxacanum* is a spreading, evergreen plant having 6-inch-long, brownish stems covered mostly at the ends with rosettes of thick, grayish green leaves. Yellow flowers appear in the spring. Hardy to 10°F.

S. *palmeri (compressum),* an attractive, flowering evergreen, has fleshy, gray green leaves in loose rosettes at the top of stems 6 to 8 inches high. Beautiful yellow flowers are produced from April to summer. Hardy to 10°F.

S. *sarmentosum* is a hardy, spreading evergreen with yellow green leaves that grows about 6 inches high. It has relatively large, bright yellow flowers that appear in profusion in the spring, covering the foliage. Hardy to −40°F.

S. *spurium* is a creeping, nearly evergreen perennial with rounded, green leaves in loose rosettes forming a 3- to 6-inch mat. Sometimes called 'Dragon's Blood', this sedum is very popular in colder sections of the country. Clusters of light red, starry flowers bloom in late summer. Hardy to −40°F.

Culture: Sedums root easily from cuttings; they even propagate themselves from broken leaves. They are not particular about soil or water; as a guide, use the least amount of water that will keep them healthy and colorful.

Uses: Sedums are, by definition, rock plants, although their use is by no means confined to rock gardens. There are species that are effective on slopes, between steppingstones, in mass plantings, as container plants, and, especially, blended with other ground covers such as the prostrate junipers.

Sempervivum
(Hen-and-chickens)

Hen-and-chickens (*Sempervivum tectorum*) is a plant well known to American gardeners, having arrived with the earliest settlers. Its leaves are fleshy and grow in rosettes. There are many varieties and cultivars displaying different colors and heights.

Culture: Hen-and-chickens is very easy to grow, requiring only sun and good drainage. Watering is not usually necessary except during exceptionally long droughts. In a good soil, growth is faster. Propagate by separating offsets. Hardy to −20°F.

Uses: Planted around rocks, hen-and-chickens quickly fills in cracks and crevices. On dry slopes it can outgrow most weeds. In medieval years, this plant was used for binding soil on the sod roofs of cottages. The species name *tectorum* is a Latin word meaning "roof."

Soleirolia soleirolii

Teucrium chamaedrys

Soleirolia
(Baby's-tears)

Baby's-tears (*Soleirolia soleirolii, or Helxine soleirolii*) is a creeping, mosslike plant that forms a dense, soft carpet 1 to 3 inches high. The foliage is composed of tiny, light green, rounded leaves growing in a tight mat.

Culture: This plant requires shade, rich soil, and moisture. It is quickly killed by direct sun, drought, or subfreezing temperature. Propagate by division, planting sections 6 to 12 inches apart. Use outdoors only in the warmest regions. Hardy to 32°F.

Uses: Baby's-tears provides a cool, delicate effect when planted at the base of trees or shade plants such as ferns, camellias, and azaleas. The plant is well named, for it is as fragile as a baby's tear. A few steps will not kill it, but the footprints will remain for days.

Stachys
(Lamb's-ears)

The herb lamb's-ears *(Stachys byzantina)* got its name from its shape and woolly softness. It grows to 18 inches high in clumps 3 feet wide. Its leaves are 4 inches long and a silvery gray color that contrasts well with green plants. Purple flowers appear in summer on 1-foot spikes.

Culture: Lamb's-ears is easy to grow, requiring only good drainage and full sun. Cold winters may damage some leaves, so plants are usually cut back in the spring. Clumps can be divided at any time of year. Hardy to −20°F.

Uses: The gray leaves of lamb's-ears stand out dramatically against the green foliage of plants such as wild strawberry. The plant also combines well with other gray-foliaged plants, including blue fescue, dianthus, woolly thyme, and snow-in-summer.

Teucrium
(Dwarf Germander)

Dwarf germander (*Teucrium chamaedrys*) is an undramatic but neat, tough little plant. Stems 6 to 8 inches high are closely covered over their full length by small, serrated, medium-green leaves to form a thick cover. Tiny, rosy lavender blossoms appear on the upper parts of the plant in the summer. Growth is rapid by spreading, underground root stems.

Culture: This plant grows in any well-drained soil and is best in full sun. It is a drought-tolerant, heat-loving plant that requires only occasional summer watering. It is easily propagated by division or cuttings; set plants 12 to 15 inches apart. Hardy to −35°F.

Uses: Left untouched, dwarf germander is effective in large, informal areas and in desert and rock gardens, where its deep roots serve as a binder in sandy soil. It takes well to shearing, often serving as an excellent low, formal hedge or walk border.

Stachys byzantina

Thymus
(Thyme, Mother-of-thyme)

Listed below are varieties of the herb thyme that are most commonly used as ground covers. There is some confusion in the naming of *Thymus*, so you may find the plants under different names at your local nursery.

These plants are characteristically prostrate or creeping; have tiny leaves opposite one another that are sometimes covered with delicate, white hairs; and produce small flowers on upright spikes. They are, above all, aromatic, releasing their delightful fragrance whenever they are rubbed or walked on.

Creeping thyme, or mother-of-thyme (*Thymus serpyllum*), forms a flat, green mat. Upright stems, 3 to 6 inches high, are loosely covered with whorls of tiny, pale lavender flowers that appear from late spring through summer. The plant is excellent as a border, in a rock garden, and also on dry slopes. It takes light traffic.

White creeping thyme (*T. s.* 'Albus') forms a denser, lower mat covered in spring and summer by a profusion of tiny,

Thymus serpyllum

white flowers. It grows 2 to 4 inches high and is excellent between steppingstones. It tolerates light traffic.

Pink creeping thyme (*T. s.* 'Roseus') is the same as 'Albus' except that its flowers are pink.

Lemon thyme (*T.* × *citriodorus*) is similar to *T. serpyllum* but with lemon-scented foliage.

Woolly thyme (*T. pseudolanuginosus* or *T. lanuginosus*) has tiny, gray green, soft, woolly leaves that form a dense carpet 2 to 3 inches high. Its somewhat mounding growth habit makes it strikingly effective between steppingstones, spilling over a boulder or low bank, or simply alone as a small accent plant. It has tiny, pink flowers that seldom appear. It takes somewhat more traffic than the others.

Common thyme (*T. vulgaris*) is coarser and taller (6 to 10 inches) than *T. serpyllum* and is better used as a low hedge. Cultivars 'Argenteus', 'Fragrantissimus', and 'Roseus' may be available at some nurseries.

Culture: Thymes present few problems. They grow in almost any well-drained soil, prefer full sun but can take some shade, and need regular watering in hot-summer areas. Beyond periodic trimming to keep them tidy, they need no other care. They are easily propagated by division or cuttings taken in the spring; set new plants 6 to 12 inches apart. All are very hardy, to −30°F or −40°F.

Uses: In addition to the plants' landscape uses, try dried thyme in stews, crush on lamb chops, or sprinkle on broiled salmon. Add thyme to any food served with white wine.

Tiarella
(Foamflower)

Foamflower (*Tiarella cordifolia*) is an attractive, deciduous perennial that makes an excellent ground cover in moist, shady areas. It is native to the woodlands of eastern Canada and the United States and is a close relative of coralbells (heuchera). The plant's lobed leaves (somewhat like maple leaves) are 2 to 4 inches in diameter and frequently offer brilliant color in the fall. Foamflower's most outstanding feature is the beautiful, fluffy clusters of flowers on 12-inch stalks that cover it in May. Although white is the most common color, pinkish, purple, and other shades of red have been cultivated. The plant spreads vigorously by underground runners.

Culture: Native to forests and woodlands, this plant prefers a moist, humus-rich, slightly acidic soil. It's best

Thymus vulgaris

Trachelospermum jasminoides

to divide clumps every 2 or 3 years. Propagate by root division in spring or fall. Hardy to −30°F.

Uses: Foamflower is a fairly tolerant woodland plant that makes a fine ground cover in naturalistic gardens, shaded rock gardens, and in small, shady niches around the home.

Trachelospermum
(Star Jasmine, Asiatic Jasmine)

Star jasmine (*Trachelospermum jasminoides*) is one of the most widely used plants in mild-winter areas, mostly as a ground cover but sometimes as a vine. It is a twining rambler with long, woody stems; handsome, oval, deep green leaves; and small, sweetly fragrant, starlike flowers that appear from early spring through summer. Its leaves are 2 to 3 inches long and its flowers ³/₄ inch in diameter.

The leaves of Asiatic jasmine (*T. asiaticum*) are somewhat broader and its flowers yellower than those of star jasmine. The alternate facing of the leaves, spaced about 1½ inches apart on the stems, adds to the beauty of the foliage. Both plants are slow to get started and slow-growing, but they are quite sturdy once established, getting woody with age. Average height is about 1 foot.

Culture: These jasmines require shade in desert areas and sun or partial shade elsewhere. They grow best in a fairly rich soil and need regular watering throughout the year. The plants are subject to iron chlorosis. Propagate by

cuttings; set rooted plants 2 feet apart in spring. Cut back upright shoots. Some weeding is necessary until plants fill in. Hardy to 15°F.

Uses: These plants are best used in small areas, such as under trees in any raised location, where they may have the opportunity to spill over a wall or serve as a landscape accent.

Vaccinium
(Mountain Cranberry, Lingonberry)

Mountain cranberry (*Vaccinium vitis-idaea minus*) is native to the northern United States and Canada, its range extending from Alaska to Massachusetts. It is a relative of the blueberry. Its leaves are about ½ inch long, evergreen, and glossy.

Flowers are white to red, bell-shaped, and about ¼ inch long. Mountain cranberry spreads by underground runners and makes a dense, even mat 8 inches or less in height. Red berries (very sour when fresh) are useful for preserves and syrups.

Culture: Mountain cranberry requires moist, acidic soil. In mountainous, cool-summer regions, full sun is accepted if plants are generously watered. Otherwise, grow the plants in partial shade. Propagate by dividing the creeping roots or by transplanting sodlike clumps. Hardy to −10°F.

Uses: Mountain cranberry is most useful in naturalistic gardens where it can become a floor for shrubs such as large-growing rhododendrons. A single plant in a garden will spread to form a small mat.

Vaccinium vitis-idaea minus

Vancouveria
(American Barrenwort)

American barrenwort (*Vancouveria hexandra*) is a Pacific Northwest native that is closely related to the epimediums. It grows to 1 to 1½ feet tall. White, ½-inch flowers appear in May through June. The leaves are light green and delicate, and they die to the ground each winter.

Culture: American barrenwort grows naturally in the shade of Pacific Coast redwoods. There, the plant's needs are well met: the soil is acidic and high in organic matter, temperatures are cool, and there is plenty of moisture. Hardy to −25°F.

Uses: This is an excellent ground cover plant where it is well adapted. Combine with ferns and epimediums around the base of trees and in shaded beds. The cut foliage is attractive in bouquets.

Vancouveria hexandra

Verbena
(Verbena)

Spectacular flower colors, a long blooming season, and a rapid growth rate make Peruvian or trailing verbena (*Verbena peruviana*) among the most popular plants used as ground covers. It is an evergreen perennial that grows to a height of 4 to 6 inches and spreads rapidly to form a dense, flat mat of green foliage composed of small leaves closely spaced along the stems. Crimson red flowers rise above the foliage in flat-topped clusters, blooming almost continuously from spring through fall.

A number of excellent hybrids between *V. peruviana* and the common garden verbena (*V. × hybrida*) offer a wide array of flower colors. Among the best generally available in the nursery trade are 'Appleblossom', with its light pink flowers that are 8 to 12 inches high, and 'Little Pinkie', whose bright rose-pink flowers bloom late into the fall. The plant is very low-growing (4 to 6 inches high) and makes an attractive ground cover with bright green leaves and a distinctly creeping habit. 'Princess Gloria' has salmon-colored flowers; 'Raspberry Rose' is a vigorous grower with large, dark green leaves and raspberry rose flowers; 'Starfire' has bright red flowers and blooms in winter in southern California.

Culture: V. peruviana and its hybrids are grown as annuals in cold-winter areas and as short-lived perennials in warm-winter areas. When grown as perennials, the plants should be cut back severely in late fall and a balanced fertilizer applied. Verbenas require hot, sunny locations to thrive and to produce the most flowers. Once established, they are quite drought-tolerant. To avoid problems with mildews and other fungus diseases, they should be watered infrequently but deeply during the summer. They grow in moist soils and perform equally well along the coast and in deserts. They are easily propagated; root cuttings planted on 2-foot centers will form a complete cover in a single season. Hardy to 25°F.

Uses: These verbenas are effective anywhere in the landscape that brilliant color is desired. The low-spreading forms are particularly useful on moderate slopes, where, planted in small-to-medium-size areas, they provide erosion control.

Veronica
(Speedwell)

The speedwells are classic garden accent and border plants. The species listed here have been chosen for their proven practicality, popularity, and different growth habits. All are evergreen perennials (in most of the country) with shiny green, notched, oval to lance-shaped leaves and

Verbena × hybrida

attractive flowers, mostly on spikes, that appear in the summer. They are vigorous, fast growers that can serve as a lawn substitute, but they do not take traffic.

Woolly speedwell (*Veronica incana*) forms a tight, 6-inch, gray green mat with pale blue flowers on spikes that rise 6 inches higher. Hardy to −40°F.

Hungarian speedwell (*V. latifolia* 'Prostrata') has a similar growth habit but spreads more widely and has dark green foliage. Hardy to 0°F.

Creeping speedwell (*V. repens*), the lowest-growing, forms a 4-inch, dark green mat dotted in spring and early summer with clusters of small, blue flowers. It makes an excellent lawn substitute. Hardy to −10°F.

Culture: These plants grow in full sun or partial shade. They need good soil and regular watering throughout the year. They are easily propagated by division.

Uses: These speedwells make good paving plants, particularly in shady areas. They can soften the edges of steps or paved areas and serve as bulb covers. Anyone who has fought to keep the weedy speedwells out of a lawn knows their potential as lawn substitutes.

Vinca
(Periwinkle)

In form, structure, and growth habit, the periwinkles (*Vinca major* and *Vinca mi-*

Vinca minor

nor) are similar. The main differences are that *V. major* is coarser, grows 3 to 4 times as high, is strongly invasive, and less hardy. Both periwinkles are evergreen trailers; they spread rapidly, with the stems rooting as they trail. The leaves are a glossy dark green, growing opposite one another about every inch or so along the stems. In the spring, lilac blue flowers appear in moderate numbers toward the stem ends.

V. major grows vigorously to 2 feet. Two-color variants having leaves mottled with white or gold are generally available.

V. minor grows to about 6 inches. The principal cultivars are 'Alba', white flowers; 'Atropurpurea', purple flowers;

and 'Aureo-variegata', leaves spotted with yellow.

Culture: Periwinkles grow best in light shade and a good, moist, well-drained soil. They can be propagated by division or from stem or root cuttings. Set divisions or rooted cuttings 12 inches apart in spring. *V. minor* grows well in any climate in the country with the exception of hot desert areas, where it grows in the shade but tends to turn yellow from high temperatures even if watered. *V. minor* is hardy to −30°F; *V. major* is less hardy, tolerating temperatures to −10°F.

Uses: *V. minor* is among the best of the evergreen ground covers, not only because of its hardiness but also because of its quiet, cool beauty. It is an excellent choice for medium-scale planting, particularly in the filtered shade of large trees or shrubs. It is also effective in raised beds or planters where it might be designed to trail for several feet.

V. major is useful as a large-scale ground cover on slopes, particularly in naturalistic gardens and around country homes. Leaves falling from overhead trees vanish beneath its foliage. It is sometimes used as a container plant for hanging baskets.

Veronica prostrata

Vinca minor

Leaves are evergreen to semi-evergreen and glossy green in color. Leaflets are smaller than those of *W. fragarioides*—about ½ to 1¼ inches long. The plant is compact-growing, with few problems.

Culture: The waldsteinias are widely adapted, easy-to-grow plants, but they do best when provided with ample water in a well-drained soil. Propagate by seeds or division; plant on 12-inch centers. Hardy to −20°F.

Uses: These plants are too frequently overlooked. They have been used successfully on banks, in rock gardens, and around homes.

Viola
(Violet)

Pansies, violas, and violets are herbaceous perennials belonging to the genus *Viola*. Pansies and violas are commonly grown as annuals or biennials; a few species of violets are useful ground covers.

Violets are 3- to 6-inch-high plants with bright green leaves and summer-blooming, ¾-inch-wide flowers in a wide range of solid and mixed colors. They grow in tufts and spread by creeping runners. The Australian violet (*V. hederacea*) forms a tight, leafy carpet heavily dotted in summer with typical violet flowers—mostly blue in the center and fading to white at the tips.

The sweet violet (*V. odorata*), the classic popular violet, has dark green leaves and mostly fragrant flowers. Numerous cultivars are available with flowers of different size and color. Among them are 'Royal Robe', with large, deep blue flowers; 'Marie Louise', which has fragrant, double, white and lavender flowers; 'Royal Elk', with long-stemmed, single, fragrant, violet-colored flowers; 'Charm', with small, white flowers; and 'Rosina', which has pink flowers.

The Confederate violet (*V. priceana*) is stemless and has large leaves up to 5 inches wide and flat, pansylike, whitish flowers with violet blue veins.

Culture: To look their best, violets need partial shade, plenty of water, and rich, moist soil. They can be propagated by seeds or, faster, by division. Violets produce copious seeds and will naturalize and spread where they are adapted, even to the point of becoming a pest. Sweet violet and Confederate violet are hardy almost everywhere; Australian violet is much less hardy (to 20°F).

Uses: These plants are best for small-scale planting—as borders, in beds, or around large-leafed evergreen shrubs.

Waldsteinia
(Barren Strawberry)

The barren strawberry (*Waldsteinia fragarioides*) is for those who admire the foliage of the strawberry but do not want the fruit. Like *Duchesnea indica*, it has 3-leaflet, evergreen leaves, up to 2 inches long, that are toothed at the tips; 5-petaled, yellow flowers; and a creeping growth habit. It forms a thick mat 4 to 10 inches high in sun or shade. It does not tolerate drought or extended periods of heat. Like other strawberry plants, it can be propagated by seeds or division.

W. ternata is best adapted to southern Canada and the northern United States. In both sunny and shaded locations, it maintains an even, 4-inch height.

Xanthorhiza
(Yellow-root)

Xanthorhiza simplicissima is an easily grown, deciduous shrub that deserves to be better known by home gardeners. It grows very uniformly to a 2-foot height.

Waldsteinia fragaroides

Toothed or lobed leaves are 1 to 3 inches long and turn a beautiful yellow orange in the fall. Drooping clusters of tiny, purplish flowers appear in May, usually before the leaves unfold. Spreading roots and stems have an attractive yellow bark.

Culture: Yellow-root is tolerant of many soils but grows most luxuriantly in moist soil. It prefers full sun but can grow in medium shade. The easiest method of propagation is to simply dig clumps, but root cuttings also can be taken. Hardy to −30°F.

Uses: This is a good plant for low, wet spots—areas for which the choice of plants is small.

Zoysia
(Korean Grass, Mascarene Grass)

Although a true grass, *Zoysia tenuifolia* is suitable for use only as a ground cover and not as a lawn grass. This is because of its tufting, mounding growth habit, which presents a lumpy surface practically impossible—and aesthetically undesirable—to mow. Usually referred to simply as Korean grass, it forms a velvety turf composed of fine, closely growing, dark green leaves 3 to 5 inches long. The turf remains evergreen wherever temperatures remain

Zoysia tenuifolia

above freezing, but turns brown at the first frost, slowly recovering as temperatures rise. Korean grass is slow to become established and spread.

Culture: The plant does best in a well-drained soil, in sun or light shade. It can grow in a heavy soil that is never allowed to become soggy. Korean grass is drought-resistant and needs only moderate watering. New plants are best started by

separating sections of root systems and planting them no more than 6 inches apart. Hardy to 20°F.

Uses: Korean grass can be used as a lawn substitute in warm climates and where a tailored effect is not desired. It is perhaps most effective in small patio settings, growing between steppingstones or railroad ties, or on a slope. It accepts light traffic.

Xanthorhiza simplicissima

INDEX

METRIC CONVERSION CHART

U.S. MEASURE AND METRIC MEASURE CONVERSION CHART

		FORMULAS FOR EXACT MEASURE			**ROUNDED MEASURES FOR QUICK REFERENCE**				
	Symbol	When you know:	Multiply by:	To find:					
MASS (WEIGHT)	oz	ounces	28.35	grams	1 oz		=		30 g
	lb	pounds	0.45	kilograms	4 oz		=		115 g
	g	grams	0.035	ounces	8 oz		=		225 g
	kg	kilograms	2.2	pounds	16 oz	=	1 lb	=	450 g
					32 oz	=	2 lb	=	900 g
					36 oz	=	2¼ lb	=	1000 g (1 kg)
VOLUME	tsp	teaspoons	5	milliliters	¼ tsp	=	1/24 oz	=	1 ml
	tbsp	tablespoons	15	milliliters	½ tsp	=	1/12 oz	=	2 ml
	fl oz	fluid ounces	29.57	milliliters	1 tsp	=	1/6 oz	=	5 ml
	c	cups	0.24	liters	1 tbsp	=	½ oz	=	15 ml
	pt	pints	0.47	liters	1 c	=	8 oz	=	250 ml
	qt	quarts	0.95	liters	2 c (1 pt)	=	16 oz	=	500 ml
	gal	gallons	3.785	liters	4 c (1 qt)	=	32 oz	=	1 l
	ml	milliliters	0.034	fluid ounces	4 qt (1 gal)	=	128 oz	=	3¾ l
LENGTH	in.	inches	2.54	centimeters	⅜ in.	=	1 cm		
	ft	feet	30.48	centimeters	1 in.	=	2.5 cm		
	yd	yards	0.9144	meters	2 in.	=	5 cm		
	mi	miles	1.609	kilometers	2½ in.	=	6.5 cm		
	km	kilometers	.621	miles	12 in. (1 ft)	=	30 cm		
	m	meters	1.094	yards	1 yd	=	90 cm		
	cm	centimeters	0.39	inches	100 ft	=	30 m		
					1 mi	=	1.6 km		
TEMPERATURE	F°	Fahrenheit	5/9 (after subtracting 32)	Celsius	32° F	=	0° C		
					68° F	=	20° C		
	C°	Celsius	9/5 +32	Fahrenheit	212° F	=	100° C		
AREA	in.²	square inches	6.452	square centimeters	1 in.²	=	6.5 cm²		
	ft²	square feet	929	square centimeters	1 ft²	=	930 cm²		
	yd²	square yards	8361	square centimeters	1 yd²	=	8360 cm²		
	a	acres	.4047	hectares	1 a	=	4050 m²		